LEAST OF THE LITTLE ONES

Tuition Centres in the Mission of Holistic Child Development (HCD)

LEAST OF THE LITTLE ONES

Tuition Centres in the Mission of Holistic Child Development (HCD)

E. David Karunakaran

2021

Least of the Little Ones: Tuition Centres in the Mission of Holistic Child Development (HCD) – Published by the Indian Society for Promoting Christian Knowledge (ISPCK), Post Box 1585, Kashmere Gate, Delhi-110006.

© Author, 2021

Online order: http://ispck.org.in/book.php

Also available on amazon.in

ISBN: 978-93-90569-08-3

Laser typeset by

ISPCK, Post Box 1585, 1654, Madarsa Road, Kashmere Gate, Delhi-110006 • *Tel:* 23866323

e-mail: ashish@ispck.org.in • ella@ispck.org.in
website: www.ispck.org.in

To

My parents Ebenezer and Dulsie

My parents in law Ravindranathan and Judith Lydia

Contents

SECTION B

SECTION C

Foreword

Holistic Child Development (HCD) has been an increasing matter of concern globally and thankfully it is receiving growing attention both in the secular as well as Christian circles. For a long time, children's welfare received only lip service and their issues were given only peripheral attention. However, taking into consideration the ever-increasing number of children, more concrete initiatives are desperately and urgently needed. Consequently, in the wake of inexpressible atrocities being brought on children due to world wars, famines, floods, communal and ethnic clashes, migration, and sheer poverty, something had to be done to protect children globally. In such a context, the United Nations Organization came forward to establish the UN Convention on the Rights of the Child which set the guidelines for the civil, political, economic, social, health, religious and cultural rights of children. The initiative of the UN certainly helped to create a sense of awareness and responsibility towards children globally.

India being part of UN treaty, is required to develop and implement policies for children's holistic development, although technically, the Constitution of India guarantees fundamental rights to all children in the country and empowers the state governments to make special provisions for children, ensuring that children are holistically protected from exploitation. However, in reality very little is being done both at the central and the state government level as India is home to 472 million children under the age of 18 years, representing 39% of the country's total population. The sheer number of children in India is so huge that ensuring the implementation of children's welfare policies proved to be a huge challenge. Consequently, most children, especially children from poor families both in the urban as well as rural India, continue to suffer.

Looking at the overall Indian scenario, we are overwhelmed to note the complexities and pathetic situations the children live in. Among them, children from rural areas, slums and urban poor families, scheduled castes, tribal communities, and other disadvantaged populations suffer from multiple deprivations. The causes for this are related to poverty, malnutrition, access to quality health services, child marriage, poor school attendance, low learning outcomes, lack of sanitation facilities, hygiene, and access to improved water. But then there are numerous types or kinds of urban children in India. These include children of affluent and rich families who are well taken care of, though they too have their own challenges and concerns. Then the children of urban middle-class families are found in our cities. These children by and large are better off as their families are able to take good care of them. However, their struggle to come up in life, and to do well in their studies to keep up their middle-class status brings a lot of stress upon them. The children living in low-income housing in cities, by and large, tend to be taken care of by the family, but the ongoing concern to come up in life with limited family resources also brings a lot of stress on them. Constant pressure from the family and society to do better in their lives tend to destroy the joy of being a child.

The next categories of urban children are of major concern in urban India. These categories include children living in slums, children living on streets, children living in shelters, remand homes, refugee colonies, homeless children, handicapped children, children of bonded laborers. Children in these categories are a big matter of concern as these children are the most destitute and yet largely neglected by the families, societies, and even the governments.

A closer look at the slums reveals that there are about 7.6 million children living in 49,000 slums of Indian cities. These children face tremendous atrocities in their lives but are also faced with complex challenges in their early childhood. Most slums have a huge percentage of child laborers as India sadly is the home to the largest number of child laborers in the world. Approximately 12 million child laborers are found in Indian cities and towns. Most child laborers are between seven and 14 years of age, toiling for 14-16 hours a day. Poverty and lack of social security are the main causes of child labor, as their families are in dire need. Hence, children are compelled to work instead of going to schools which they cannot practically afford. Even if they are enrolled in the school, they drop off soon due to the circumstances they live in. Generally, children dropping out of school end up as the child labor force. Then there are street children in India that are largely found in cities. Most street children are inadequately protected, supervised, or directed by responsible adults. It is estimated that more than 400,000 to 800,000 street children are found in cities of India. These children come to live on the streets and take on the full responsibility of caring for themselves. They are often exploited by employers and the police. Most children who leave home to live on the streets come from slums, poor families, and broken homes. High illiteracy, drug use, alcoholism is prevalent among them. They are vulnerable because of lack of access to nutritious food, sanitation, and medical care.

Although Christian churches and missions organizations have been involved in traditional ministry to the children, the changing context of India demands the change in their overall approach in dealing with children. While carrying on the traditional ministry to children through hostels, schools, orphanages, and other means, some fresh thinking is emerging as to how to keep the holistic child development in mind while ministering to them. Among the Christian theological circles, child theology has been emerging as a discipline and many Christian NGOs are dealing with issues like 'children at risk, 'child labour' 'children's rights', child abuse, child stress, gender discrimination, etc. This is an encouraging sign, however, issues related to children are to percolate from theology to praxis, so that the neediest children would benefit from it.

In this context, Dr. David Karunakaran's initiative in writing a practical and insightful book on Holistic Child Development is noteworthy. He is passionate about the subject as he has been deeply involved in Holistic Child Development in the city of Chennai and in Odissa. Having come from the grassroots level, he demonstrates a real heart and concern for the Holistic Child Development throughout his research and writing. While various efforts are being made to develop children holistically, Karuna's approach through tuition classes perhaps is more innovative and practical as it has impacted and prepared children to sustain their studies well and move forward in their lives. It is not unusual that children who are weak and slow in studies lose their interest in schooling. This is where the strategic importance of tuition centers is seen.

Dr. Karunakaran believes that tuition centers can provide a missional platform to facilitate Holistic Child Development. To prove his point, he provides numerous stories of how these tuition centers have helped numerous children to come up in life. The approach provided by the tuition centers is practical and workable, therefore it facilitates Holistic Child Development in the slums of India in a significant way.

This book provides a substantial basis for Holistic Child Development that is biblical as well as practical. While providing useful information about various aspects of Holistic Child Development and especially integrating tuition centers with a missional goal, Dr. Karunakaran has provided an innovative, practical, and comprehensive model of mission through tuition centers. I commend this book to those who have a heart for children, especially vulnerable and needy children living in thousands of slums of India.

Rev. Atul Y. Aghamkar, PhD
Former Professor and Head, Department of Missiology
South Asia Institute of Advanced Christian Studies, Bangalore
Director, National Center for Urban Transformation

Preface

God has been indescribably gracious in enabling me to bring out this book which is an outcome of my experiences in serving children. About ten years of working in a Children's home, and another ten years in Odisha, has been a time of gaining awareness on the ground realities of children ministries. In this book, I have attempted to bring to light issues related to children ministry and tried my best to find a way forward. I am neither a scholar nor a theologian but an ordinary Indian follower of Jesus Christ. I reflect the concerns of many servants of God who carry the burden for the need of transforming the lives of children at risk. This is an urgent and ardent call for churches and missions in India.

A few years before the commencement of this century, I took up managerial responsibility of a Children's home that had been running for more than twenty years. Within few years, a historical paradigm shift was introduced by the foreign funding agency to all the partner organizations running children homes in India. A deadline of five years was declared. By the end of the five years, all the partner organizations in India were expected to close homes and take up child centred community development projects. The alternative was an end to the partnership, and thereby, the funds. It was a challenge. Training programs were arranged, in the meantime, by the funding agency for the capacity building of partner organizations to undertake community-based projects for child development. Very few of the partner organizations running children homes, funded by this agency, came forward to implement the change. Many preferred to change partnership in order to continue the Children's homes or close them.

During the five crucial years, I was fully committed to adopt the changes introduced by the foreign funding agency. New staffs were recruited, tuition centres were opened in churches, awareness programs were conducted in schools, survey for need and capacity analysis was conducted in villages, and contacts were developed with government departments, industries, and other NGOs. Consequently, funding continued, all for the sake of chid centred community development. In spite of these progresses, unfortunately, the organization I was working with could not come to a firm decision as it was struggling to find answers to the questions - Is closing Children's homes and going to community work God's will? Why should we close homes when it has been an opportunity to lead children to Jesus for years? Can we, the children of God, work with village leaders and government officials who are not Christians, but corrupt? Does the Word of God permit it? Will they allow us to evangelize their children as we do in homes? If not, why should we work for their children?

At the same time, from the experiences of the newly launched child centred community development programs, though short-lived, I had gained first-hand knowledge about the vulnerable situations of children in villages and slums. I was faced with some difficult questions. Why should I do this community work? For the sake of funding agency or is this the will of God? What if my organization decides to stop community programs? Who will then serve children at risk in the absence of outside funding?

The Church is the answer. It dawned on me that every local church in India is responsible to serve children at risk in its vicinity in every possible way. This is what Jesus taught through the story of the Good Samaritan. The lesson Jesus wants us to learn from the Priest and Levite is more relevant for the Church in India today. This sight of new horizon led me to look for a way to serve children at risk with the available local resources. The booklet of Luis Bush on 4/14 Window was an eye opener that eventually brought me to the highway of Holistic Child Development (HCD).

Without my knocking, God opened the door of doctoral studies in SAIACS. The research work I had undertaken among tuition centres in slums was so enlightening that the objectives of substantiating relevance of tuition centres in children's ministry and developing a model tuition centre facilitating Holistic Child Development have been satisfactorily achieved. All those findings are put together in this book.

I express my hearty gratitude to Dr. Y. Atul Aghamkar for readily accepting my request to write the Foreword for this book. His mentorship was highly supportive throughout the journey of my thesis writing. I am thankful to Dr. Jesudason Baskar Jeyaraj for providing me with resources on HCD. I am thankful to Sridharan Kalistas who encouraged me to publish my thesis as a book. My heartfelt thanks to my brother in Christ, Philip Inbaraj, General Secretary of Faith Good Works Fellowship who has provided every moral support in times of need.

I thank Stephen Ravindran, my brother in law, who met the needs of this publishing. My hearty thanks are due to ISPCK for coming forward to publish this title. Let me also thank you for buying the book.

It is my sincere prayer that God may bless this book to be a tiny spark of inspiration for churches and mission organizations to serve children in India.

E. David Karunakaran
Thiruninravur
Chennai

A GLANCE

*Relevance of Tuition Centres
for the Mission of HCD in Slums*

Chapter 1

Multidimensional Challenges to Child Development in Slums

Imagine a world where you bathe with only a bucket of water. Wash your kitchen utensils and bathe your children on the streets in front of your house. Do the laundry of your entire family with two buckets of water. Go to railway tracks or banks of stagnant water pool to release yourself. One room to cook, sleep, study, store all your household items, and occasionally bath in a corner of the same room. Imagine trying to sleep after a long night shift amidst the blaring sound of TV or the endless noise of coughing of the old man in the family living next door. This is slum life. And more sometimes.

Memories of our childhood days remain with us throughout our life. It is, after all, one of our most cherished times. At the same time, we cannot deny that there are millions of children whose future is at stake. They live at the risk of losing their childhood bliss of safety, growth, and joyful times. They are disappointed when they look for a model life they would want to emulate. They are ignored when they ask questions, their dreams shattered before they even take flight. The impact of this childhood lingers throughout their life affecting every relationship throughout their life. Taking a walk through any slum, one cannot shrug off the sight of crowded single room houses with lanes less than five feet wide. How would we feel if we had lived our childhood there?

Slum living makes children highly vulnerable to losing what God intends them to be. They encounter multidimensional challenges every day in every aspect of their life. When family, school, neighbourhood, peers and community at large surround a child in slum, it exerts an enormous negative influence on the child's overall development. So, a multidimensional ministry is the need of the hour. To fulfil this purpose the concept of Holistic Child Development is found to be a relevant mission tool for churches and mission organizations. *HCD has in focus spiritual, physical, cognitive, and social development of children.* "And Jesus grew in wisdom and stature, and in favour with God and men" (Luke 2:52).

This book is the outcome of a study of tuition centres in Chennai slums. Tuition centres provide a mission platform to facilitate Holistic Child Development (HCD). A mission tuition centre model that facilitates HCD in slum context is recommended at the end. Except in illustrations and unless otherwise mentioned, wherever you find 'Child' or 'Children' it implies children in the context of slums. In the present age of information, technology based on electronic science, the clarion call to the Church and its mission is to reach out to children in the most vulnerable environments. Slum children are just an example of millions of children in different contexts of risks in India, living in need of *missional intervention that is holistic, relevant, contextual, compassionate, sustainable and transformational.*

Understanding Slums

A slum is defined as a compact area of at least300 population or about 60-70 households of poorly built congested tenements in unhygienic environment usually with inadequate sanitation infrastructure. A slum is also called 'Cheri' in Chennai, 'Chawls' in Mumbai, 'Bustee' in Kolkata, 'Peta' in Andhra, 'Keri' in Bangalore and 'Katra' or 'Galli' or 'Jhugii' in Delhi.

According to a survey taken in 2014 there are 2173 slums in Chennai with a population of 10,42,337 (www.timesofindia/ timesindia/Chennai-slums). This accounts for 28.89 per cent of the total population of Chennai. From 2001 to 2014 an increase of 51.85% in slum population has been reported. A constant growth of slums is predicted in days to come since many families abandon rural agrarian lifestyle and are attracted by livelihood opportunities created by Special Economic Zones around cities. This is a mission challenge as the state of children in slums is alarmingly vulnerable.

Causes and Effects of Slums

The lack of financial capacity of migrant labours from villages to buy land or house in cities is the major cause of slum formation. Government should be able to provide facilities for prices affordable by these migrants. Unfortunately, it is not the case. Poor labourers are exploited by proprietors of companies and factories. Political forces are another cause for slum formation. This dilemma drives them to settle in any available space, like the roadside, river banks or any open space that belongs to no one except the Government.

Many explanations are given for the migration from rural to urban. Migration is not harmful when it is managed well by the Government and the community. As a matter of fact, migration for economic reasons and for better livelihood is profitable for the people in terms of access to education and improved standard of living. Migration is also an attempt of the rural poor to break the confines of caste and other extreme deprivation.

Are slums untouchable? In general, there is a stigma about slum dwellers. Such an attitude needs to be changed for effective mission among the children in slums. From the socio-economic point of view, slum people are "resources" not "burden". They often provide goods and services to the non-slum population.

A statistical report says about 51% of slum families are from Scheduled Caste and Tribes. In rural situations, these families suffer greatly from suppression of upper caste people and landlords. In slums they are free from traditional bindings of religious affinity. Their mind would be tuned to receive new ideas for spiritual, social, and economic development.

Having a problematic environment in slums does not rule out the fact that there are some positive aspects too. Children in slums have better access to schools. Parents know for certain that the future of their children depends on the educational ladder they climb. So, they want to make use of every opportunity to achieve this end. While most children access to government schools in the cities, some go to matriculation schools also.

In slum living, one can say, childhood is poisoned at its very source. That means, children are deprived of most of the five core ingredients of Holistic Child development (HCD) namely, security, boundaries, significance, community, and creativity. We will have a look at the challenging life realities of slum children with respect to their Spiritual, Physical, Cognitive and Social development.

Challenges to Spiritual Development
In this section, we will look into a couple of slums in Chennai. This will help us gain some ground realities to the challenges of HCD of slum children as such.

Let us first consider a slum in Chennai. We will meet some children and parents to find out what it takes for them to live in squatters. People and conversations in the following pages are purely fictitious. They are meant to bring before us the realities children in slums face.

Family Traditions

As we entered, we came across a man in a black *dhoti* with bare chest. He appeared to be in his early 40s. He was an ardently religious man. Photos of about ten deities could be seen in the room. He said he was getting ready to go to Sabari mala. This is a place in Kerala where the temple of the deity Ayyappa is located. We started a conversation with him,

"When are you going to Sabarimala?"

"Tomorrow and tonight we have a special *poojah* in our house. Please come and join us."

"Why you are going there, may we know?" He smiled at us and replied with pride, "This is our family tradition. Right from my grandfather we keep up this practice every year. This time I am taking my 12 year old son with me."

"What about your work on such days?"

"That is not a big problem. I take loans from pawn brokers on interest for all these expenses. We need the blessings of god Ayyappa, that's all."

Every year the number of Ayyappa devotees going to Sabarimala keeps increasing.

In a slum family, what a child mostly experiences are superstition and ardent religious practices which are cultic. The cultural force is so strong that it might take years for the children to practice their faith in Jesus Christ independently and openly.

We moved on and took a break in a tea shop. The shop keeper gave us a friendly smile and handed over our cups of tea. We asked,

"Any Christians here?"

"There are two families going to church."

"You are not interested to go?"

"No, no, it does not suit me. They ask us to remove jewels, wear only white clothes. In our culture, only widows wear white sarees. And names must be changed. How can we change our culture?"

Identity Loss

On 10th August 1950, the then-President of India signed and issued the Constitution (Scheduled Castes) Order, 1950. According to this order, a SC person who becomes a Christian loses the benefits he/she was entitled to before. For this reason, it is predictable that parents may prevent their children from going to church or prayer meetings.

Lack of Reading Skill

There was a Tamil Daily on the wooden bench in front of the tea shop. We called the boy looking at us from the house opposite where we sat.

"Hello what's your name?"

"Ajith"

"What class are you studying in?"

"9th class"

"Come, can you read this heading in the newspaper?"

The boy blushed. He signalled by his hand that he could not read.

A research known as Program for International Student Assessment (PISA) undertaken in 2009 revealed that students in Tamil Nadu are not in a position to read and comprehend literature.

**Table 1: Percentage of Students having
Proficiency in Reading Literature**

	% at or over baseline
Himachal Pradesh	10.8
Tamil Nadu	17.3
OECD Average	81.2
Shanghai-China	95.9
South Korea	94.2
Finland	91.9
USA	82.4
Brazil	50.4
Indonesia	46.6
Mexico	59.9
Turkey	75.5
Argentina	48.4

Not being able to read literature curbs the capacity of children to read the Word of God and grow spiritually. It is one of the real challenges to spiritual development of slum children.

Challenges to Physical Development

Addressing the problems of physical health of children is a vital part of mission. Physical development of a child is endangered where favourable environment for physical wellbeing is lacking.

Housing and Sanitation

The primary threat to physical welfare of children in slums is the lack of proper housing. First of all, the one room houses that they live in is a temporary one. They could be asked to vacate anytime by the government or by any political tycoon. The plights of slum children without toilets and drainage facility are distressing. It is highly probable that slum children get attacked by diarrhoea, pneumonia, jaundice, fever, dysentery, skin diseases, worm infection, eye and ear infection, and stomach-ache. Children, moreover, grow under the constant threat of domestic violence.

At the next street we saw a woman climbing from the end of the street with an empty brass water bowl in her hand. The noise of a plying train so closely indicated that a railway line was just behind the houses. The area they used as an open toilet.

There was a girl washing vessels just in front of her house. We looked at the 'colourful' water in the bucket.

"Why is this water so colourful?"

Then girl replied without looking at us.

"This is the water we get in the street tap. We have complained to the corporation a week ago. They promised to come and check it."

Unclean water is another major cause of challenge to physical welfare. In slums, water is found alarmingly contaminated due to mixing of sewage water with drinking water in pipelines. It is no wonder that most of the diseases in slums are water born.

Suddenly we heard loud noises of shouting of a man and wails of a child. As we walked towards the house, we saw a man beating his child of 6-7 years with a leather belt.

We appealed to him, "Please do not beat the child"

Breathing heavily the father spoke, "No, Sir without a beating he will not learn. I spent five hundred rupees for doctor's appointment and medicine just yesterday, that too I had borrowed. Today he wants to go out to play with his friends"

Nearby, a vegetable vendor called aloud.

We looked at the bamboo basket in his bicycle. We noticed that the vegetables were all half spoiled ones.

Further along, we saw a petty shop. As we bought some bananas and ate it, a girl walked to the shop, bought a soap, and ran off.

"Why isn't the girl in school?" We enquired the shopkeeper.

"She is the daughter of a relative of mine. She was studying in 8th class but now she looks after the house as her elder sister got married a few months ago. She does the cooking and looks after her 2-year-old brother as both her parents go to work."

"How she can do these things being a child herself?" we exclaimed.

The shopkeeper agreed. "True, but there is no other way. A couple of days back she fainted and fell on the street while carrying water from the tap. She is now ok."

Then the shopkeeper turned around to tie bunches of neem leaves above the doors beside the shop.

"What is this?" We asked him.

"My child has measles. If I do such *poojas* he will be alright"

"Such diseases are from viruses. It has nothing to do with *poojas*." We smile at him.

He did not seem to mind us saying so and replied, "I don't know, Sir. This is our belief system."

Challenges to Cognitive Development

We soon moved out of the slum and as we were about to cross the road, we met a friend of mine who was a teacher in a government school nearby.

"Hello! How are you? Why are you here?" he asked.

"We came to see if we could be of any help to these children"

He seemed pleased with the idea. Filled with much hope, he began to pour out his heart.

"Please help them to continue school. They also need help with their homework. Last week a studious boy stopped coming to school. I learnt that he is now working for a contractor in a company. His parents want to save money for his sister's marriage. I had hoped that he would graduate and turn his life around." He took a long pause after saying this.

"Another girl who was a rank holder is now getting ready for marriage." His face turned sad. While we were conversing, two men passed by. One stood before the first house and the other at the doorstep of the next house. We could hear them yelling, "Who is there? Come out." They took out what appeared to be notebooks and turned the pages. We turned to the teacher for an explanation, but he spoke before we could ask.

"They come for collection of interest for loans borrowed by the families."

"Does this happen often? Monthly or weekly?"

"Sometimes daily. It depends on the urgency of the matter. Eventually, the interest would be twice or thrice the loan amount. Debt cycle is the major cause of economic distress that affect development of children every way."

With heavy hearts, we said goodbye to the teacher friend.

We realized that prayers are not enough, and we also had to do something ourselves.

Apart from family circumstances, there are shortcomings in the schools too, that contribute to impeding slum children's education. The quality of teachers is one of the major concerns here. It is alarming to note that in the Central Teacher Eligibility Test (CTET), 11.95 percent of candidates cleared Paper I exams meant for teachers of classes 1-5 and only 2.8 percent cleared Paper II meant for teachers of classes 6-8. Inprivate schools, these teachers cannot get placement. In government schools, quality of teachers is measured generally not by performance or aptitude but by government approved certificates provided by teachers training institutions. In Tamil Nadu there are number of teachers training colleges functioning with approval of the government where money often plays a central role in getting approval and admission of students as well. Students getting admission are also mostly guaranteed of getting appointed as teachers in government schools. Moreover, being appointed in government schools provides job security that rules out viability of any disciplinary action against irregular attendance and insincere performance.

Challenges to Social Development

People immediately conclude that there is a closer proximity towards social evils in a slum environment. This is irrefutable. In general, slums stand for dissatisfaction and discontent, empty stomachs, hands without work and mind without occupation. There is an undeniable close relationship between slums and crimes. Children of criminals in prison or parents under court trials face hostility and unfriendliness of neighbours and relatives. If an adolescent girl eloped with a boy, it would make the future of younger girls in the family, if any, highly questionable. Threats of suicide are quite common in slums. Parents or adolescents attempt suicide for various reasons. Debts, family quarrels, illness, failure in relationships, extra marital affairs, failing in school exams are some reasons. Children undergo psycho-social trauma causing depression if such incidents happen in their families.

Adolescent girls are most vulnerable to social challenges. They can fall prey to emotional drives intuited by adolescence. There are several instances where a young impressionable girl comes in close contact with a boy, and begins a relationship, in the event of her finding personal love and care that appears to be lacking in her family. No longer wanting to remain a burden for her parents, she elopes with the boy. By choosing this way of life, she denies herself education and development to be a respectable and responsible person as seen in the society. Generally, girl children are seen as a burden because of dowry system in marriages. For this reason, parents are very calculative in spending for their daughters' education. Often, in many families, only if the girl's education has scope for becoming a means of income for the family will parents consider spending money for her education.

India has stepped up from being in the 108th place in 2018, to 112th in 2020 in Gender Inequality Index. Out of 153 countries where Council for World Economy had made the research, gender inequality level in India was found to be 66.8%.

For adolescent boys, slum living could be disastrous. Whenever there is a theft case in the city or any other crime report, the immediate attention of police turns to slums. Tamil cinema has produced few films exclusively on slum life. Watching these films, ridden with violence and mafia networking, viewers can get an idea of how a child's development is under constant threat in slums.

In schools, slum children are likely to experience caste discriminations. Children are referred to as 'our group children' and 'other group children.' A teacher of high caste would show partiality towards Scheduled Caste children. In this way, children from slums are mostly side lined by other children and teachers alike. But children from slums are necessary for running the school that provides salary to teachers. Slum living is generally blamed for slow learning, poor attendance, unfinished homework, and failing in exams. This raises the question: How can we, the church of Jesus Christ, then, help the least of the little ones living in slums to see a bright tomorrow?

From the perspectives we have come across so far, we can conclude that as the Church of God, redeemed from sin to do good works and good works only, something needs to be done for the children. That 'something' needs to be something more than traditional Song, Story and Scripture approach. That is where

Holistic Child Development comes into the picture. It is a well proven mission strategy. It is not a strange idea. It is near and clear as we catch hold of God's concern for children. "For it is by grace you have been saved, through faith-and this is not from yourself, it is the gift of God- not by works, so that no one can boast. For we are God's workmanship, created in Christ Jesus to do good works, which God prepared in advance for us to do" (Ephesians 2:8-10).

Chapter 2

Mission of HCD in Vulnerable Contexts

A young man in his teens was finding it exceedingly difficult to be on time for work in a factory in Chennai because his village was too far off from the factory. A Christian working as supervisor in the same factory came forward to help him by letting him stay in his home which was closer to the factory. So, this young man stayed with the Christian family, well known to me, for a couple of years. He hailed from a staunch Hindu family practicing several religious rituals like keeping silent whole day, looking at his own palms when he wakes up from bed etc. Despite such a lifestyle, the Christian family treated him as one of the family members. They never forced him to read the Bible or pray while they certainly kept praying for him to know Jesus personally. In due course, under their tutelage he qualified himself as a diploma graduate in technical education and left for Bangalore to pursue his own career. As the true story was narrated by the Christian, it was such a surprise to know that the young man became a follower of Christ and married a Christian girl despite oppositions from his family. He is now a committed member of a church in Bangalore, actively involved in ministries. The unconditional and holistic Christian love shown to the youth yielded fruit in time. This could be an exemplary practical case leading to understanding Holistic Child Development mission.

History holds that most Christians, pastors, church and mission leaders, ministers and missionaries are people who have taken the life decision of following Jesus Christ before the age of 14. However, the context today is different from their childhood days. In the 21st century context, children face vulnerabilities of greater severity and this is still greater for poverty stricken children.

Vulnerable Situations

United Nation Convention on the Right of the Child (UN-CRC) has defined and declared the four rights of the child as mandatory for its member countries. They are Survival right, Protection right, Development right and Participation right. Any circumstance that causes threat to these rights creates vulnerable situation for the holistic development of the child.

Survival right of a child explains the right of a child to live right from the time of conception. Female infanticide, caring for pregnant women, children of unwed mothers, pre-natal and post-natal care, and nutritious food are some of the issues related to Survival right. Further, the basic needs of clean water, healthy food, hygienic house, and environment also count for ensuring Survival right of a child.

Any form of child abuses like physical, mental, sexual abuses, trafficking, child labour and neglect is violation of Protection right. Physical abuses include beating, harsh punishments and refusal of food, clothing and shelter. Mental or emotional abuse is related to scolding, threatening, usingfilthy language, cursing, negligence of due attention in times of illness, failing to keep promises, failing to provide schooling requirements and any activity that curbs the child's dignity and confidence as a human.

Development right of the child demands that opportunity and accessibility are in place regarding education, skill development, training in various disciplines of choices and careers that is essential for a self-sustaining life.

Participation right gives the child freedom of expressing likes and dislikes. A child needs to develop in a social set up where the child gets accustomed to live in a social set up of sharing opinions and views. Vulnerability prevails where and when these rights of the child are not complied with in family, school, or community.

HCD and 4/14 Window

Practically speaking, HCD is not a newly invented concept. In 1983 the Nazarene Compassionate Ministries began to serve children holistically around the world without being attached to any concept or title. Though it is not possible to trace out the history of HCD concept as such, we can understand that the dawn of the 21st century brought in Christian focus on HCD. In 2000, HCD took a form of theological course. In May 2007, a Global Consultation on HCD was convened at Chiang Mai, Thailand. This historical event gave way to the formation of Global Alliance for advancing HCD. Since the year 2000, a Post-Graduate degree course on HCD has been offered in Malaysia Baptist Theological Seminary. Theological base of HCD and equipping churches on HCD ministries are the two core objectives of the course. Further information regarding networks and resources can be obtained from the internet ID given in the bibliography.

A foundational explanation of the concept of HCD as a mission to children in vulnerable situations particularly in 10/40 Window countries was provided by the mission strategist Luis Bush. He called the mission strategy "The 4/14 Window."

10/40 Window represents countries geographically located between latitudes of 10 degree and 40 degree in the upper hemisphere of the globe. These are the countries least evangelized. Even though incidents of persecutions due to religious extremism are not unusual in these Asian and African countries, number of followers of Jesus have increased exponentially. Now, the most urgent mission challenge of the Church in 21st century is 4/14 Window in this 10/40 Window.

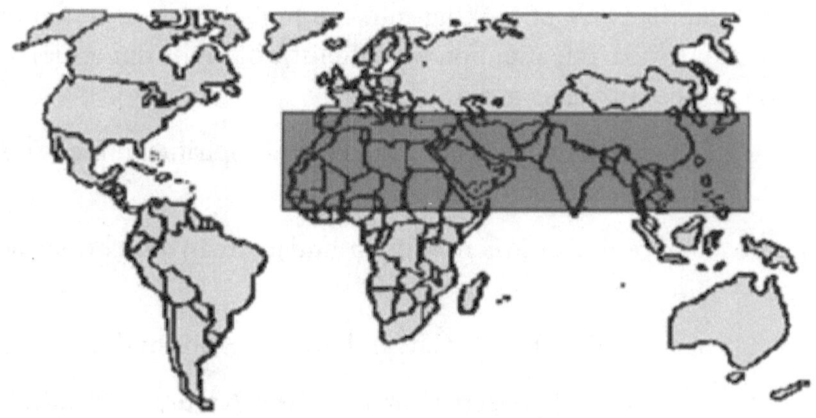

Map showing 10/40 Window Countries

4/14 Window means children in the age group of 4-14. This is the crucial formative period of a person. Bringing children in this stage to Jesus is the most challenging task of the Church and its Mission today. Patrick Johnstone, author of the book *The Church is Bigger Than You Think,* as quoted by Luis Bush, pinpoints that there are 'five challenges' to be considered in this mission task among children, namely Urban, Social, People, Ideological and Spiritual. It is well predicted that by the end of 21st century, 80% of the population will be living in urban settings. Urbanising will certainly give rise to formation of slums. And children in slums are the main concern of this book. HCD is the need of the hour in mission to such children. A staggering estimation of more than 56% of children in the world living in dire deprivation and 37% of children living in acute hunger calls for missional intervention by the Church.

Holism

Mission originated from God right from creation. Prior to the fall of Humanity into sin, God, Humanity and Nature were in harmony. From the way God created the universe and humankind, we can know clearly that God purports it to be holistic in relation to each other. Another way of looking into the holistic nature of God's Mission is to turn our attention to the holistic or multi-dimensional consequences of sin as given below:

1. Separation between God and Human-Spiritual dimension of consequence of sin

2. Separation between Human and Human-psycho-socio dimension

3. Separation between Man and Woman –Social dimension

4. Separation between Humanity and Nature – Physical, Economic, and Cognitive dimensions of the consequence of sin

5. Separation between Nature and Nature- Environmental dimension

If so, the mission of God must be an all-inclusive task of redeeming the whole universe back to its original state of sinless, glorious, and eternal fellowship of the Triune God. "We know that the whole creation has been groaning as in the pains of childbirth right up to the present time. Not only so, but we ourselves, who have the first fruits of the Spirit, groan inwardly as we wait eagerly for our adoption, the redemption of our bodies" (Romans 8:22-23). Again Paul points out the culmination of God's plan of redemption as "to put into effect when the times will have reached their fulfilment-to bring all things in heaven and on earth together under one head, even Christ" (Ephesians 1:10).

Child

A child is not the property of parents. Just like God is the owner of all the creations, he is also the owner of children though children are born through parents. What God wants us to know about children can be put in the following lines.

1. Being in the image of God, children are human in full, yet they need to be instructed.

2. They are a source of joy yet exhibiting sin.

3. They are susceptible yet capable.

4. They are models of weakness and immaturity yet used by God.

Every child is unique, valuable and bears the image of God. God reveals himself in a child. Children must be accepted and treated equally with dignity irrespective of their caste, creed, sex, colour and living environments. Childhood is a strategic stage to reach out in the process of developing a human into an adult in God's purpose. It is worth quoting here the lines of Dorothy Law Nolte:

If a child lives with *criticism*, the child learns to *condemn*

If a child lives with *hostility,* the child learns to *fight*

If a child lives with *ridicule*, the child learns to be *shy*

If a child lives with *shame*, the child learns to feel *guilty*

If a child lives with *encouragement*, the child learns *confidence*

If a child lives with *praise*, the child learns to *appreciate*

If a child lives with *fairness*, the child learns *justice*

If a child lives with *security*, the child learns to have *faith*

If a child lives with *approval*, the child learns to *like himself/ herself*

If a child lives with *acceptance and friendship*, the child learns to find *love in the world*

Development

Is the idea of 'Development' unspiritual? Not so. Generally, we Christians use the term 'Blessing' to denote life growth as received from God. 'Development' can be the same. Children, as God's blessing, can be seen as closely related to development of family and community and nation too. In turn, God holds accountable the family, community, and nation for the development of children.

God announces blessings for Zion in terms of children's well-being. "The city streets will be filled with boys and girls playing there" (Zachariah 8:5). Development is both successes and failures. Development is more than economic growth; it is humanisation whereby people are freed from poverty, ignorance and physical ailments. Christian view of holistic development of children has spiritual formation at the core and the goal of development would be becoming more like Jesus Christ in whom values of the kingdom of God are manifested expressively and fully. True development leads to self-sustainable support that contributes to development of others. A child scoring good marks in Mathematics after coaching by a tutor will assist another child get good marks in Mathematics. That is development.

Stages and Theories of Child Development

Children are generally divided into groups of beginners (4-5), primary (6-8), junior (9-11), intermediate (12-14) and senior (15-18). The present book focuses on the HCD of children in the age group of 6-14.

Primary Children (6-8)

Children in this group love to be with others and long for a secure family environment. They develop a curiosity about things around them asking questions with inherent honesty. By the age of 6, children come to the awareness of gender difference.

Junior Children (9-11)

Imaginations enrich this life period. Children in this phase read and exhibit good memory capacity. They yearn for role models and become hero worshippers easily.

Intermediate Children (12-14)

This is a transition period from late childhood to early adolescence. Children struggle to gain control over their behaviour. A strong quest for finding answers set in. Sexual drives develop and attraction to opposite sex shows off. Children in family conflicts are most likely to fall prey to love affairs.

Freudian Theory

The founder of psychoanalysis Sigmund Freud (1856-1939) developed a theory of psychoanalysis in 1896 that keeps sexual instinct as basis for human development along with parental treatment as an influence for child development. He explained child development with three elements, namely Id, Ego and Super-ego; Id operating on pleasure impulses, Ego on real and rational instincts and Super-ego on decisive factor of human behaviour. The five stages of child development proposed by Freud are Oral (birth-1 year), Anal (1-2), Phallic (2-6), Latency (6-11) and Genital (11 onwards). Hence the age group of 6-11 is understood to be a time of preparatory life.

Eric Erikson Theory

This theory provides a theoretical framework to understand emotional development of children. He proved that childhood experiences influence adulthood. Five stages of child development proposed by Eric are Hope (0-1), Will (1-3), Purpose (3-6), Competence (6-12) and Fidelity (12-18). On comparing, it is found that Eric's theory is closer to the Christian understanding of child development than Freud's.

Christian and Scientific Views of Development

While secular understanding of development is materialistic with human at the centre, Christian view of development is spiritual and holistic with God at the centre. Spiritual disposition determines development. In the spiritual realm, sin causes curse, and curse, if not removed, sustains poverty. Jesus Christ is the only Way to overcome sin and curses. There is no possible way to deal with curses in a secular approach since secularism does not count on sin. Only the Christian way of engaging in holistic development alone can bring true changes to alleviate poverty and its consequences.

Paradox of Eschatology and Development

Christian faith looks forward to the culmination of the world order at the second coming of Jesus Christ. In terms of general perspective, eschatology refers to the end of the world and in terms of personal or individual perspective, eschatology refers to the death of a person. In that case why should we be concerned about the non-spiritual well-being of children? Is not teaching spiritual truths enough? The model of Jesus Christ is the answer. He preached salvation and practiced social action. Christian development work rests on the resurrection power of Jesus Christ. It is undertaken in obedience to the gospel to glorify God emphasizing on the anticipated reality of the Kingdom of God on earth. Otherwise, failing to involve in developmental social action limits the content of the gospel.

Teachings of Religions on Themes Related to HCD in Slum Context

Sensitivity to Multi-Faith Context

Children in Chennai slums grow in families of different religions. While engaging in mission among these children one needs to be cautious about the reality of the multi-faith culture in existence there. 'Indian Christianity' is the need of the hour. Children showing a positive response to gospel are to be cautiously nurtured to live with unbelieving parents. Wise methods of communicating the gospel to the children in the local cultural context are to be considered. An awareness of local beliefs and religious practices is paramount in the Church for an effective communication of the gospel. Children differ in their responses to the gospel. Some may do so immediately, and others may take time. Children not responding immediately must be prayerfully and patiently counselled. They are not to be treated indifferently.

Knowing about the teachings of major religions of Christianity, Hinduism, Islam is quite profitable to understand the children and facilitate their holistic development as a mission. Five themes are chosen: Spirituality of children, Poverty, Sufferings, Casteism and Gender. What these three religions teach on these five themes is presented below.

Spirituality of Children

Christianity

Are children sinful? Do they need salvation? Do children need to believe in Jesus Christ for their salvation? According to Christian belief every child is born sinner due to 'Original Sin.' And we know that Jesus loves children. He did not find them a nuisance to his ministry or his time of rest. The Bible clearly says that children need to be taught God's commandments in every possible occasions (Deuteronomy 6).

Spiritual nurturing will be the base for the overall development of children's personality.

Hinduism

Children are held in high esteem in popular Hinduism. However, this is not without bias within the system of *varnas* viz. castes. A child enters into spiritual life as he/she is twice born when the ceremony of *Upanaya* is performed. However, this is not permitted for *Sudras* and *Panchamas*, who are suppressed as 'untouchables'.

In mystic Hinduism sacrificing children was believed to be necessary to appease demons. Such superstitions are most likely to influence the parents in slums longing for prosperity who are willing to do anything to attain it. Very scarcely we come across media reports of child sacrifices.

Islam

Islam holds that children are given by Allah to be cared for and reared in the knowledge of Allah. A new born child is so precious for the family that they immediately recite in the ears of the infant the basic creed of Islam: "*La-Ilaha-Illallah, Muhammadur Rasullullah*" meaning "there is no god but Allah, and Muhammad is his apostle." Islam does not teach about original sin, but it indoctrinates on 'minor sins' and 'major sins'. For Islam, any act that is against the teaching of Allah is sin.

Poverty

Christianity

The Bible says it is God who made both the rich and the poor (Proverbs 22: 2; Proverbs 17:5). God is pleased with the service to the poor and rewards them (Proverbs19:17). The Bible also points out that poverty is better than falsehood (Proverbs 19:22) and that hard work can alleviate poverty (Proverbs 20:31). Hence, Christianity views poverty not as a curse but as a way of life that is miserable and yet can be overcome with self-determination and outside help.

Hinduism

Hinduism believes that everyone has his or her own destiny; no single faith can suffice to lead them into liberation. With this, Hinduism explains poverty, suffering and destitution to be the result of sins in earlier births or previous lives. According to Hindu belief it is the fate of the individual to have been born in poverty and it is the chance of next birth that will solve the problem of poverty.

Islam

Islam teaches that believers of Allah must show concern towards poor and needy. An annual savings called *Zakah* that is 2.5 per cent of unused funds is to be strictly made available for charity purposes.

Sufferings

Christianity

Children in crisis show us the reality of suffering and pain as a signpost in the process of fulfilling God's will on earth. The life of Jesus Christ has established a new paradigm of suffering. Christianity's view of the problem of suffering is explained well in the life and sufferings of the cross of Jesus Christ. Suffering can be a means of glorifying God. Submission to sufferings makes one walk closer with God. Spirituality sharpens through sufferings.

Hinduism

Through Karma theory combined with belief in rebirth, Hinduism explains that sinners suffer either in the present or in the next birth, and as such, the righteous prosper either in the present or in the next birth. Also, in the four stages of life, namely Student, Husband, Hermit and Ascetic, the last two stages naturally impose sufferings in order to fulfil the duties of birth and attain salvation.

Islam

Quran teaches that though God permits sufferings, in order to strengthen and purify the faith of followers, sin could also be the reason for sufferings. There are two types of convictions among Islamic theologians; one holds God responsible for sufferings and the other counts humankind responsible. However, Islam requires its adherents to do good works to relieve others from suffering.

Casteism

Christianity

Caste system and hierarchy came into Christianity through the converts of dominant caste communities. Otherwise Christianity knows no caste as the gospel propagates equality. There is no favouritism with God (Romans 2:11).

Hinduism

Hinduism is known for caste disparities. Based on the Hindu scripture a child enters into the society through the rite of 'twice born' performed when the child is eight years old. Only the children of the first three *varnas* of *Brahmins*, *Kshatriya*, and *Vaishyas* are eligible for the twice-born rite. For *Shudras*, serving the above three *varnas* is the only way to salvation. People not included within these four *varnas* are equal or lower than 'cows' which is considered as a sacred animal.

Islam

Islam does not teach about sects or casteism as in the case of Hinduism, but divisions came into existence for political reasons only after Muhammad. There are two broad sects of Islamic followers namely Sunnis and Shias. Shias are further divided into more sub-sections.

Gender

Christianity

The Bible teaches that God created humanity in his image as male and female (Genesis 1:27). M.V. Tilak ascertains that man and woman are two sides of one coin with respect to their inner life. Yet when it comes to the point of roles and responsibilities men are opted for authority in home and eldership in church with the attitude of a humble servant, which is in contradiction to worldly pattern. Both men and women are equally valuable before God. Christianity does not propose superiority of either man over woman or the other way around.

Hinduism

In Hinduism, to be born as a woman is a form of punishment for the previous birth. The woman has no role in any religious practice and her most important duty is to take care of her family members. In Vedic tradition, special prayers were offered to get a male child. Girls are considered a burden even in many present Indian societies mainly due to the system of dowry. This worldview leads to illegal abortion of female fetus.

Islam

There is no place for gender inequality in the Quran. This means that in the spiritual realm both man and woman are viewed equal before God. It was in the medieval period of eleventh century A.D. when women were first marginalized in the name of traditional orthodoxy.

We can, then, conclude that the goal of the mission of HCD is understood to mobilize local churches to engage in the ministry of transforming the present age children particularly in vulnerable contexts into future transforming agents of the communities they belong to. The challenges related to religion, culture, psycho-socio-economic are turned to be stepping stones to achieve the goal.

Chapter 3

Tuition Centres as Educational Mission

All through the history of missions, education has predominantly occupied a central stage. Few glimpses of history of teaching and mission schools provide an interesting backdrop that projects tuition as an appropriate mission activity. This can be one of the strategies for future mission in India just like educational institutions of yesteryears. That means for a mission minded Christian, tuition or teaching is not only a profession but a mission.

Jewish Tuition

For a Jewish child, family is the primary place of learning. A child received education in an informal environment of his/her home. Education was imparted basically through religious instructions. On becoming four years old, the child is expected to recite from memory the prayer of *Shema* that is Deuteronomy 6:4-9. Parents were the tutors. Parents were responsible for the development of children to be good and righteous. With fellowship of God as the central focus, children were tutored to be happy with good characters. While the mother tutors girls in house making, the father tutors boys in a trade for livelihood. Apostle Paul is said to have been trained in tent making by his father.

During the era of synagogues, the place of Jewish worship, children were tutored in reading, writing and arithmetic. Priests took the role of tutors in synagogues. From here developed scribes whose reverent responsibility was to write down the Book of Law, the first five books of the Bible known as Pentateuch. From 64 B.C. a universal system for primary education in synagogues was introduced. According to this children, of six years were admitted in the primary schools called 'Beth Hassepher' (House of Book) in synagogues all over the world where there was a Jewish colony. Children of age 10-15 were tutored to know 'Mishnah' well by heart at 'Beth Hammidrash' (House of Study).

Christian Tuition

Christian faith has an indispensable part of tutoring or teaching. As the gospel of Jesus Christ was spreading, new believers were to be tutored on the teachings of Jesus Christ. Followers of Christ gathered in houses to worship. These were the earliest **House Churches** of Christian tuition, we can say. House worship had two parts. In the first part, tutoring of believers on the instructions of Jesus and apostles were carried out. Those teachings were known as *missa catechumenorum*. In the second part, Eucharist service was conducted. Later **Catechumenal Schools** were established where bishops or priests or laymen tutored students both young and old, on ways of Christian living. Question-answer method was adopted for tutoring. Individual attention was given. There were two stages a believer was to pass through for one or two years before becoming a full member of the church.

In 2nd century A.D. **Catechetical Schools** appeared in prominent cities of Christian populations like Alexandria, Jerusalem, and Constantinople, to train and develop leaders of the Church. Subjects included philosophy, dialectic, history, Greek literature, rhetoric, arithmetic, geometry, music, and astronomy.

Children and Tuition in Ancient Tamil Society

Tolkappiam and *Thirukkural* are two collections of poems of ancient Tamil literature written by two different poets namely Tolkappiar and Thiruvalluvar respectively. The origin of *Tolkappiam* is approximately dated around 300 B.C. to 1 B.C. and that of *Thirukkural* is later than that of *Tolkappiam* but not after A.D. 200. *Tolkappiam* reveals that children in ancient Tamil society were treated as treasures of family and they were enjoyable, bringing harmony and happiness in families. He also affirms that education was accessible for all irrespective of gender, religious and caste differences.

Thirukkural extols childhood. It compares the sound of musical instruments with the sounds made by children and concludes that the latter is most desired. Out of 1330 maxims, 10 are about children. About having the pleasure of children, Tiruvalluvar writes: *Of all the treasures cherished the most precious is none other than the birth of gifted children* (*Thirukkural*-61). On the development of children, Thiruvalluvar writes: *Prodigy of children gladdens the hearts of parents and enlivens all mankind(sic) on earth* (*Thirukkural*-68).

Education in ancient Tamil society did not owe allegiance to any religion. Caste and gender discriminations entered Tamil society in later ages. Brahmins introduced Casteism-*Varnashram*- in the name of divine statute. Out of four varnas starting from the top *Brahmins*, *Kshatriyas*, *Vaishyas* and *Shudras*, children of the only first three varnas were educated. Children of *Shudras* and of *Panchamas* who were treated as untouchables, were strictly prohibited from education as per the divine oracles of the Vedas.

It could be ascertained that there were three types of schools. One was Family School. The teacher would come to the homes of each student and teach. The other one was House School. Students would go to the teacher's house. The front portion of the house was set aside to accommodate students. The third one was

Gurukul school. Students were expected to stay with teachers in ashrams and learn. Children of the least in the caste ladder were not supposed to learn. This was the state of education in Tamil society when the first Protestant missionaries Bartholomaus Ziegenbalg and Henrich Pluetschau, two German theological college graduates, sent by the King Frederick IV of Denmark, arrived at Tranquebar, in the South Eastern coast of Tamil Nadu on 9th July 1706.

Early Mission Schools

The beginning of the missions of European Christianity in India commenced with the arrival of Vasco da Gama, a Portuguese sea-voyager, at Calicut in Kerala on 17th May 1498. In the following years, Goa became the centre of Roman Catholic administration. On 6 May 1542, Francis Xavier, a Roman Catholic Jesuit priest who was a Spaniard, landed at Goa. On knowing that fisherfolk communities in south Tamil Nadu were eager to embrace Christianity he visited a greater part of the coastal villages between Cape Comorin (present Kanyakumari) and Tuticorin (present Thuthukudi) of Tamil Nadu. He ran a school where he taught Parava community children (fishers) the precepts of Roman Catholic Christian faith. Those children were asked to teach the same to their parents.

While Roman Catholic missionaries were teaching children to memorize prayers and confessions of faith, Ziegenbalg, the first Protestant Lutheran missionary to India and Asia as well, arrived at Tranquebar in 1706 and founded a school in 1707 to teach children to read and write in Tamil. The aim was to enable them to read the Bible by themselves. Importance was given for Christian education of reformed teachings of the gospel.

18th Century Mission Schools in Chennai

Society for Propagation of Christian Knowledge (SPCK) was the pioneering mission to start charity schools in Madras (present Chennai). With the sponsorship of SPCK, missionary named Johann Ernst Grundler started a mission school in Black Town,

Madras, in 1715. Due to practical difficulties it was closed for 10 years. In 1726, missionary Benjamin Schultz reopened the school. Number of students increased from 12 to 35 students in the year 1729. This is the school now famously known as St. Paul's Higher Secondary School in Chennai today.

Lutheran missionary Johann Philip Fabricius along with another missionary Christian Wilhelm Gericke started a mission Boarding school in Madras in the year 1787-1789. By the year 1828, 21 mission schools in Madras were catering to the educational need of about 1000 students.

St. Mary's Church Charity School was one of the early mission educational endeavours in Chennai that started with 18 boys and 12 girls in the year1715. It was the first mission school founded by the Church of England in India. In 1903 it was moved to Poonamallee High Road and in 1954 it was renamed as St. George's School.

19th Century Mission Schools in Chennai

The span of 1813-1833 is known as a Period of Elementary Schools in India. Triple 'R' of 'Reading, Writing and Arithmetic' was the focus of mission schools where children were taught in their mother tongue. An account of mission history states that in the year 1890, out of 11,490 children in schools only 1,443 were from Scheduled caste communities and again out of 1,443 students 1,176 children studied in mission schools in the cities of Madras, Kancheepuram and Thiruvallur. Schools were meant to be a means of communicating gospel to children and through children to parents.

Christ Church School in Mount Road was founded in 1842. The strength of the school was 69 in 1850. It rose to 120 in another two years. As an extension, another mission school for poor children was started in 1874 where education was provided free of cost. The present-day St. Matthias' Anglo Indian Higher Secondary School had its beginning as a Lower Primary School in 1891. Later in 1912, it was opened to the education of children from poor families with provision of scholarships. As a measure of serving the poor children this school was providing noon-meal to children.

The school that was opened with 57 students in Black Town of then Madras in 1837 by John Anderson from the Church of Scotland, had developed to be Anderson Rajagopal School at George Town (changed name of Black Town) today. In the beginning stages, parents of high castes stopped sending their children to this school due to the presence of low caste children. Yet, the work continued with the devotion of missionaries to develop children without any discrimination.

The following schools were started for boys: Wesley School in Rayapetta, St. Paul's and Fabricius Schools in Vepery and Kellet School and Harris School in Triplicane. Schools for girls were also started: Bentick in Vepery, Northwick in Rayapuram, Methodist High School in Rayapetta, and St. Ebbas School in Sullivan Garden.

In 1857 administration of British India was taken over by the British government from British East India Company. Schools received grants from government and missionaries were engaged in the work of supervising the schools. Christian education took prominent place in schools. Admission of students irrespective of gender, caste, and religion paved way for the spread of gospel in particular and social transformation in general. By the turn of the 20th century, education was quite accessible to all sections of the society.

Emergence of Private and Government Schools

In due course of time, some of Hindu high caste affluent leaders came together to form educational associations to run schools parallel to mission schools in Chennai. There were two reasons for this. One was the wave of social reformation spreading in Tamil Nadu. Traditional bindings of Hindu society in the name of religion were breaking down. Such radical issues as Children welfare, women freedom, annihilation of casteism, and development of marginalised communities were redressed. Schools were started for all children irrespective of caste discriminations.

The other reason was Christian education that was made compulsory in mission schools. Parents of Hindu high castes did not like mission schools' imposing Christian education on their children. Soon an amendment in education policy was brought by the Queen Victoria in 1858 that called for restrictions of Christian education in mission schools. Grant from British government was denied to mission schools that did not to implement restrictions in Christian curriculum. This caused closure of quite a number of mission schools. Missions moved to villages and started schools where there was no hindrance for Christian education.

The aftermath of Independence in 1947 saw government's vigorous action to eradicate illiteracy in the State. Mid-day meal program was introduced in schools. Later on it was enhanced as Nutritious Meal program. There are, at present, 153 primary schools, 42 high schools and 19 higher secondary schools in Chennai. About 95% of the students in all the schools come from slums. Despite various schemes launched by Chennai Corporation, the light of holistic development of slum children is very dim.

Contemporary Tuition Centres in Chennai

It is not unusual that children who are weak and slow in studies lose their interest in schooling. In order to push children up in the ladder of academic qualification, parents look for assistance of tuition centres. Hundreds of tuition centres can be found that are run in the houses of the tutors. As we walk through the streets of Chennai, name boards of tuition centres can be seen hung over the gates of houses. Some even advertise that 100% success has been achieved. Children in matriculation and Central Board curriculum are targeted so that a solid income is guaranteed. Slum children are usually not welcome here. These centres are meant for rich families. Most of the tuition centres are income oriented. Subjects that can fetch good income are concentrated more than other subjects.

Some schoolteachers gather children in their houses for tuition. This fetches extra income. Parents prefer these tuition centres as they expect that children in the tuitions run by teachers will be promoted to next class. Tuition centres in slums run by housewives or young graduate girls are purely viewed as a self-employment. Crowded footwear of children outside a house can indicate the presence of a tuition centre in that street. Prescription of fees will be comparatively less. However optimum profit will be achieved with more number of children. Many parents are not concerned about the crowd and quality of tuition. They are content with the time spent by their children in the tuition centre. In the case of both parents being employed, children are safe in tuition centres till the return of parents, particularly, the return of mothers from work in the evening.

Table 2: Components of HCD and Tuition Centres

No	Agency Classification	Components of HCD included in tuition centres	Components of HCD lacking in tuition centres
1	Churches	Spiritual Cognitive	Social Physical
2	Christian Mission Organizations	Spiritual Cognitive	Social Physical
3	Organizations of other faiths/Secular Organizations	Physical Cognitive Social	Spiritual

The above table indicates the role of tuition centres facilitating HCD. While the tuition centres run by churches and mission organizations concentrate on spiritual and cognitive development of children, NGOs of other faiths/secular organizations, focus on all the three components of HCD except spiritual component. What is required is a mission tuition centre that facilitates all the four components of HCD.

Chapter 4

Rethinking of the Church and its Mission among Children at Risk

In Odisha, we were walking out from a village one morning, after visiting children in a tuition centre. As we were about to start the bike we heard somebody calling us.

"Stop! Stop! Sir!" We could hear their shouting from quite a distance. Two villagers were coming towards us.

I became quite nervous. Why they are chasing us? Could it be some threat to stop the mission tuition centre? Should we ignore them and leave? The Odiya missionary with me asked me to stop.

Those men reached us and started talking to the missionary. I waited for the translation and soon the missionary told me, "He wants to be baptized."

I was simply wonderstruck and asked, "What do mean? Is it true?"

The missionary confirmed that one of the men wanted to be baptized.

Then I asked the missionary to verify why he wanted to be baptized. After a few seconds of conversation, the missionary said, "It seems he is in need of some money."

In India, generally Christianity is viewed as a 'rich religion' today. The general public have a notion somehow that Christians are for the welfare and development of Christians only. The rumour that Christians are funded by Western Christian countries like America to replace Indian cultural heritage with Western culture is spreading. This certainly accelerates harvest of political gains by religious fundamentalists. In view of nation building amidst challenges of poverty, corruption, economic crisis, and social evils, the question of Christian response is one which churches and missions cannot afford to ignore.

We need to begin from the roots. Church means People of God; Disciples of Jesus Christ. According to the Scripture, the term 'Church' never meant 'Buildings'. Unfortunately, it has become an accepted misuse today. Christians in India, commonly, deem it to be a blessing to contribute generously for buying land and building 'churches.' One can see the pride in showcasing different views of the big church buildings in the calendars, magazines, wall hangers, posters and show case photo displays.

Misquoting verses from the books of Ezra, Nehemiah, Haggai and Zechariah, as expressing the heart of God for church buildings, supplement to the misuse of the word 'Church'. In certain places of South Tamil Nadu, congregations celebrate anniversaries of inauguration of church buildings, parish halls, bell towers, and parsonages with much pomp. A spirit of competitiveness among neighbouring churches is said to be the driving force. If only at least half of the money spent on buildings and interiors were invested on children, think of what a transformation it could bring in the lives of children, families and the church!

There are thousands of churches of various denominations in Chennai today. A preliminary survey reveals that the churches in Chennai often lack ministries to facilitate HCD. Less than 5% of 70 parishes of a renowned denomination in Chennai engage in any form of HCD ministry. In the case of another mainline church organization it is learnt that less than 10% of churches in Chennai are doing HCD ministry.

Church and Children

The Church is the representative of God in caring for children. In other words, the Church is to reflect the heart of God for children, more particularly for children at risk. It is commendable that the Church takes every effort to prepare Bible lessons for Sunday school and VBS. Let it be. But when was the last time we heard a sermon on children in vulnerable situations? On special occasions like inaugural and valedictory programs of VBS, Children's Sunday, Christmas and Sunday school rallies, child centred sermons are most welcome. Giving importance to issues pertaining to children in vulnerable contexts in Bible as well as in society today in the sermons can keep the Church on alert about doing the best for the children. It is imperative to have a policy of setting apart a good portion of annual budget towards HCD ministries to children at risk.

It is the responsibility of the Church to educate parents on child rearing. Christian parents from disadvantaged communities like slums need proper teaching and counselling on parenting. Parents need counselling on abortion, birth control, child psychology, issues of adolescence, balancing career and children, and spiritual formation. Yester-year practices of having more children, adopting harsh punishments for disciplining, giving food on the condition of reciting Bible verses or hymnals by heart may not be suitable for child rearing today. There are Christian parents who want to send their children to schools run by Christian management which may be located quite far when there are good schools close by. This will affect children's worldview particularly, of Christian faith in relation to social life.

God's mandate for the Church is to serve children not in part but fully, holistically. During one of my preaching ministries at Christmas in a church I have known for years, I noticed a section of children were sitting on the floor separately while children of affluent families filled the choir seats. The children on the floor were from the children's home run by the church management. Their parents were certainly not part of the church congregation! And it was quite evident that the church choir did not have a place for the least of the little ones. When it was taken to the notice of the choir master he nodded with some hesitation. A year later, he promptly informed me that the Church Committee permitted him to include those children for forthcoming Christmas Carols.

Just think of the joy and dignity those children would have experienced when they were part of the choir! It is nothing less than exploitation to make it compulsory for those children to attend VBS and Sunday Classes but not considering them for choir! It is high time the Church understands that its mission among children living in poverty, that leads to highly vulnerable environment like slums, involves not only traditional routine approaches but more so in caring for their holistic development.

Children make the Church functions colourful by rendering special performances of dances and singing on the stage. Are their lives colourful? Today's newspaper, as I write this, informs the death of a school boy who committed suicide just because his parents could not afford to buy him a smart phone that he needed for online classes during the Covid 19 lockdown days. Does the Church care for the children holistically?

Another avenue of taking care of children by the Church is its partnership with the government. The Church can take up the ministry of advocacy regarding making policies and implementing schemes related to HCD. Christians in rural and urban locations can be educated on the Constitution of India, roles of government in facilitating child development and the processes of accessing to government provisions for education and other concessions related to children. For instance, it is said that funds available with the minority welfare department of government to be dispersed for education of Christian children remains unclaimed. Church can bridge the gaps. The topmost priority is to be given by the Church right now, to appeal to the government to revoke the 1950 Presidential Order that deprives Scheduled Caste Christians from availing various concessions for their children's development. The new Education Policy 2020 published by the central government of India is on the floor now for open discussions. An analysis of the policy by the Church would be certainly contributing to the children since hundreds of schools run by the Church in Tamil Nadu are funded by government.

Sunday School Ministry

In 1780 Robert Raikes founded the first Sunday school in England to minister to the children in the factories of Gloucester. As he, being the editor of Gloucester Journal, was moved by the poverty cycle, he wanted to teach the children reading, writing, arithmetic, and biblical morals so that they could get over poverty one day. Later on the Sunday school ministry led to the transformation of the nation.

Today's Sunday schools aim at nurturing children towards spiritual growth only. Glenn Miles asks, "Are those of us who are primarily concerned with children's spiritual needs taking into consideration the physical, emotional and socio-cultural needs of children?" Both social and spiritual implications must be aimed even now like the first Sunday school movement model. Dr. Razouselie Lasesto puts it rightly, "Children ministry must go beyond the Sunday school ministry. Their total welfare must be addressed by the Church".

Apart from mainline denominations, there are a number of para-church organizations involving in children ministries systematically. International missions like Scripture Union, Youth for Christ and Child Evangelism Fellowship reach out to children in schools and churches through well-organized events like puppet shows, audio-visual programs and music. Moreover, families and friends talented in storytelling, singing, musical performance and enacting evangelistic themes organize themselves as children ministry teams. They can be hired to conduct gospel programs in churches, villages and mission fields. On the other hand, the question remains 'who will attend to a child's educational, health and psychosocial needs?'

Vacation Bible School (VBS)

Generally, Children's Christmas is a annual Sunday school program. Gifts are presented to children who attended Sunday school the whole year. Best performers are honoured. VBS can be called as the annual Sunday school mission festival. VBS is held during summer holidays. The first VBS was conducted in the year 1952 in the town of Kovilpatti with 72 children. VBS provides opportunity for children of other faiths to come and listen to the gospel. It is good to see children who come to VBS start coming to Sunday school after their summer vacation. As a matter of concern, competitive spirit influences the organizers, particularly among different denominations in rural areas, regarding money spent for food and snacks, transportation of children, audio-video systems, stage arrangements, dresses and special food on the final day program. Through VBS the Church has an opportunity to connect to children at risk. Instead of spending on transportation, VBS can be organized in villages where children live.

Church's Perception of Children in Poverty

Teaching that it is God's will that his people be prosperous and healthy is a paradox. Bible clearly indicates living in flourishing prosperity and unfailing health does not mean God's blessing and neither is it God's curse when life meets tragedy and illness. However, it dominantly teaches to care for poor and needy. "Religion that God our Father accepts as pure and faultless is this: to look after orphans and widows in their distress and to keep oneself from being polluted by the world" (James 1:27).

One of the reasons why churches often do not address holistic development of slum children is the belief that poverty is the result of the individual's sinful life. This is a myth. While poverty can be a problem of sin, we must not forget the truth that the poor are victims of social injustice. The church, being a part of the society and called to witness 'in' the world, must be ready to give poor children unconditional love and care that every true Christian enjoys in Jesus Christ. Broken relationships are at the root of poverty and holistic mission is fundamentally about restoring relationships. Churches, in addition to evangelism, should consider engaging in a holistic mission among the urban poor children. Strictly speaking, HCD is more than mere evangelism.

Caring for the poor reflects God's concern for them. The Church must realize that God has provided it with resources like buildings, water, electricity, people and finance so that poor children are served generously. Incongruously Jesus' saying that poor will always be there in the world (Jn 12:8) is misquoted by many Christian leaders. Consequently, it is taken for granted that concern for poor is not a mission agenda for the Church. Theologically, such ignorance is viewed as the Church's cruelty on the life of the poor, almost as bad as blaming them for their poverty.

The need around slum children is so great that the part that the Church plays for the development of the poor is not yet adequate. The growing misery caused by the evil of poverty is the challenge that the Church has to respond from the gospel viewpoint. The church seldom cares to know about the Save Our Souls (SOS) calls from the deprived and disadvantaged children. Thomas Swaroop contends, "The challenge for the Church today is to be sensitive to hear the cry of her children. Those in most churches have little idea about the circumstances in which the poor children live and know little about the exploitation which traps children and families in poverty."

Children outside the church

While I was serving as the manager of a Children's Home in the outskirts of Chennai, the funding partner Red en Kind (REK) of Holland introduced a paradigm shift in the policies of child care projects. Residential child care programs were to be replaced by community based child care programs within the stipulated time. Under Child Centred Community Development (CCCD), program tuition centres were organized for children in rural locations. During one of my visits to a centre, I saw a girl of about 10-12 standing alone in a corner.

I asked her, "What's your name?" And she replied at once.

Then I asked, "Do you like your school?" She immediately said, "Yes."

Then I asked what she liked most in the school and what she did not. Finally, I asked her, "Do you like your family?"

She looked at me and put her head down.

"Now tell me what you want?"

She said, "I want no fighting, no quarrelling, between my father and mother."

I know a child evangelist in Chennai. Years ago, she was assigned with the responsibility of counselling students in government schools living in villages. It was a child project program in a Christian NGO. During her classes she never mentioned anything that is connected to Bible, prayer, church or Jesus. Once she told me that after a class, a few students came to her and asked, "Aunty, are you Christian?" Doesn't that question convey a million messages to us Christians who are taught by God clearly about good and bad, justice and injustice, salvation and condemnation, heaven and hell and judgement of God at the end?

There were instances, the child evangelist says, many adolescent girls in government schools averted committing suicide or eloping with a boy after having cordial talk with her. All such true stories show that there is something different that God wants the Church to do apart from mere evangelistic agenda for children.

One more instance would make the point clearer. For creating awareness among school students on HIV-AIDS we arranged for a preview meeting where the power point presentation of the lessons was screened to officials of the District Education Department and Headmasters and Assistant Head Masters of seven government schools. The Chief Education Officer seemed to have understood that we were all Christians with names like Paul, John, James, David and Mary from the NGO. After an hour of presentation, at the end, the comment the officer came up with was, "Why don't you do this program in all the high schools in this district?" What this experience shows is something serious for the Church to consider for the benefit of thousands of children.

Michael Duncan writes, "Community concerns and projects done in a prophetic and radical way will create a new set of questions in people. These questions give us an opportunity to give a reason for the hope that is within us." Church should be able to come forward to reach children inside as well as outside faith community for their holistic development. Moreover, children in the church have Christian parental care while children outside do not.

Centrality of Church Campus

Few decades back the children development projects organised by an international Christian mission were affected by government's intervention to the extent of closing them down. One of the reasons for such a drastic outcome is government's suspicion regarding running the project inside the church campus. It was seen as a subtle attempt of conversion. Why, then, were churches not willing to change and go to communities for running the children development projects? Church campuses have facilities like hall, electricity, water and serene environment and it is convenient for conducting programs. But the basic principle of mission is to go out to where people are. Meeting with children where they feel at home will be an appropriate strategy for effective mission.

The idea of house churches are being conceptualised in missions in India. Pentecostal churches can be found in and around Chennai at the rate of minimum one in every kilometre. People gather in houses or in market places or in sheds on the house roofs. In the wake of the national level lock down since March 25th 2020, due to the pandemic of Coronavirus causing Covid 19 disease, every faith family have started worship services at home. Sermons, songs and prayers are taken to the families through online electronic communication technology.

Mission Dichotomy

Another confusion that churches are faced with is about the relationship between evangelism and social concerns.

Spiritual care AND Social care?

Spiritual care OR Social care?

Only spiritual care?

Only Social care?

It all depends on the situation. Place, time, people and circumstances will determine what is to be done and when. John Stott affirms that the diligence of a pastor and a gardener are one and same. What clarity! It is natural to see spiritual and social aspects of children development as mutually complementing and interdependent. It is unnatural to separate them. Parables of Jesus subtly testify that spirituality is inherent in social life and social life is the expression of spirituality. 'Preach the gospel at all times, if necessary, use words' is the famous truism of St. Francis of Assisi.

We are reminded of the story of the Good Samaritan. Jesus told this story in reply to a question, "Who is my neighbour whom I must love?" There has been a tendency to interpret the Good Samaritan as Jesus, robbed traveller as sinner and so on. Caution is to be taken not to spiritualize this story. Here we must consider the two more people Jesus mentions. A Levite and a Priest. By pointing to these two religious men, Jesus teaches that God does not want the local churches to avoid caring for children's holistic development.

Communal Oppositions

We are concerned that India has undergone vast changes in the political, economical and social realms. Presently, many argue that the people of India have given the ruling power to those who want to make this country Hindu Rashtra. Can we carry on the Great Commission of Jesus Christ in our mother land anymore? Can we lead children in vulnerable life situations to Jesus who is the source of life in all its fullness?

It has become alarmingly common to hear about threats and prosecutions against Christians involved in ministries. Some years ago, I learnt that children in a village in Tamil Nadu were prevented by communal extremists from going to VBS. This is but one example.

Let me recall what happened in Odisha about ten years ago. When we approached villagers in Harbanga Block of Boudh district for initiating tuition ministry for their children, they resisted immediately.

"Why do you want to help our children?" they asked.

"We see they need help," we responded.

"But you are Christians," they retaliated at once. Their faces betrayed their fear of persecutions against Christians. They frankly let out their point of view, "You will try to convert us and we will be beaten by Hindus."

Khandhamal district where Christian persecutions took place in 2008 is just 3 kms from the Harbanga border. After a week, the community leaders allowed us to do our work with the condition that no prayer or telling about Jesus should be part of the tuition. It took four years for the parents to allow prayers in the tuition centres. VBS was conducted after seven years. Now Sunday Class ministry has been introduced in two villages. Sowing has commenced.

What is the reason for the change of mind of the parents? No prayer. No gospel. No songs. I am unmistakably convinced that it was the Christian witnessing through good works for the development of little children in the villages that brought about a change. Good works are part and parcel of spirituality. That is the clarity. After a few years, to our surprise, we received invitations from other villages to start tuition ministry in their respective villages as well. When the world outside the church bears enmity towards the gospel, 'doing good' will keep the world silent as it is read in 1 Pet. 2:15.

Foreignness

Christianity in India is still seen as an extension of 'White Religion and Culture.' This is mainly because of financial ties and lack of the Church's interest in learning about the religious and cultural history of India. Depending on foreign funds for child care ministries are questionable today. Several children development projects funded by foreign Christian foundations like Compassion International, Red en Kind and Kinder not Hilfe (KNH) have come to an end. Yet, plights of children around us remain to be addressed.

There are 1874 churches and 3000 Christian Institutions in Chennai according to the report of Church Growth Research Centre, 1999. For a church, concern for mission must be the imperative goal. Leslie Newbegin says, "The task of ministry is to lead the congregation as a whole in a mission to the community as a whole, to claim its whole public life, as well as the personal lives of all its people, for God's rule." Moreover, running tuition centres with local contributions is more impressive and influential than using foreign funds. The Church needs to grow to be people oriented and be involved in facilitating HCD of children.

Not only in terms of finance, even by the way children ministry is designed, foreignness is evident. For example, take the colourful pictures in the flash cards used for narrating gospel stories to children. Often, the pictures of white people and children are found in the flash cards. In addition to having life stories of famous white missionaries like David Livingstone, Hudson Taylor and William Carey in children ministry curriculum, churches can bring out life stories of Indian missionaries in regional languages. Testimonies of early Christians in India who experienced humiliations of various dimensions from their own kith and kin should be told to children.

Regarding Indian history of religion and culture, forerunners of Indian Christian Theology like Nehemiah Goreh, Sundar Singh, A.J. Appasamy, P. Chenchiah, and V. Chakkarai, P.D. Devanandan and M.M. Thomas, have provided adequate insights of Christianity in the light of Hindu spirituality. In the past couple of decades, the advent of St. Thomas in India has captured the attention of researchers and scholars. The outcome of their studies on archaeological findings, Hindu temples, sculptures, worship rituals, literatures, epics and theology, reveals that there is a very close resemblance of early Christianity in Saivism and Vaishnavism, the two major sections of classic Hinduism. It is high time the Church make use of the information in the mission task among children and youth in particular. Giving the living water of Jesus in the clay cups of Indian soil will do much favour in getting rid of foreignness in Christian witnessing.

Welfare to Development

For centuries, churches in India were involved in the welfare services of children. It is imperative that now onward development concepts are to be learned and applied for the holistic development of children. During Christmas and Easter, churches actively engage in distribution of Biryani packets to children in the neighbourhood. Every summer, the organizing committee would plan for lunch to children all the days of VBS. Such gesture of love and care for children by one time feeding is certainly commendable. Some churches even provide educational items like notebooks to the children. Once I had an opportunity to attend a church program of distributing school stationary in a village. I asked the children to write a few Tamil words on the black board. No student could do that successfully. All these children were studying in village government high schools. They not only need stationaries but guidance for studies. This is development ministry. Development ministry involves considerable participation of target people by way of mutual consultations. This approach will be helpful in proving that Christian mission is not allurement as alleged by communal fanatics. Education can be a central agenda in development ministry.

Knowledge on Holistic Child Development

For ministering to children, the Church needs to update the knowledge on HCD. Without knowing what children living in vulnerable situations undergo in their life, proper intervention is not possible for HCD. Churches in Indian context are seldom encouraged adequately to undertake research activities. Seminars on HCD in churches that develop parents, children ministry workers and missionaries in HCD mission can be resourceful.

Let us consider at least one program in a year on understanding children in the Church as well as outside the Church. Child specialists in the fields of education, health, psychology, skill development, spirituality and parental care can be invited to church programs. They can help enlarge the perceptions about children and their development. Such learning can certainly lead us to focus on issues and ways of addressing them. Neighbours of the congregation who are people of other faiths, and parents of children outside church may also show interest to participate in such meetings on child rearing.

Absence of foreign funding does not mean shutting down of children care ministries. The local churches are still capable of doing something if they are willing. All we need to do is to keep the congregation informed about the needs. Urban churches today have improved in terms of economic status due to increase in average income levels of the congregation. People are willing to give so long as regular updates are given through pamphlets or newsletters and WhatsApp and Facebook etc.

Churches must utilise resources both movable and unmovable, for income generation activity instead of disposing them for one time advantage. Another aspect that needs attention is the utility of funds. Priority should be given to investing on children in need instead of lavishing on celebrations, buildings and furnishings.

Number Game of Missions

One of the mission leaders and the founders of Christian Institute of Management, Ebe Sunder Raj in his paper presented at the Mission Consultation Conference at Chennai in 2018, pointed out that the prevailing competitive trend of mission organizations must end. The number of children committed for missionary call, attending church services, regular Sunday schools, need not be taken as the indicator for the success of the ministry at the end of children camp program. Target fixing leads to all sorts of unspiritual, unscriptural perceptions about the Church and its mission. It will commercialize the commitment. What is seen around in Christian mission and ministry, quite often, is a scenario of developing **Consumerism** that handily helps crowd pulling. But what is necessary is taking holistic care of even just one little child and that will be glorious in the sight of God.

Every church could become a tuition centre. Children both inside and outside the church can develop holistically through the interventions of tuition. In Chennai, several churches and mission organizations run tuition centres in slums.

Theological Education

Our discussion on engaging in mission to children for their HCD will be incomplete without having a glance at the theological education of Colleges and Seminaries. As far as I know there is only one college in Kerala that is offering a separate course on HCD. More and more research work needs to be undertaken by the students on children in various contexts. The society we live in needs Christ-like contemporary citizens for which theological colleges can do their best by producing graduates who will in turn be catalysts in the Church and society. One of the goals of theological education could be producing quality film makers, journalists, counsellors, entrepreneurs, leaders of people and politicians. We can say that radical reformation of theological education particularly in relation to HCD is the need of the hour. Addressing the issues of children with proper theological understanding alone will make God-honouring future leadership in the Church and in the nation out of the children today.

Setting out

Compelled by the realization for the need of HCD mission, a study was initiated to analyse the role of local churches and mission organizations in facilitating HCD through tuition centres in Chennai slums.

The questions that moved the study forward to the goal of developing a mission tuition centre are:

1. What is the significance of Tuition—viz., teaching, educating, guidance and caring- for HCD in vulnerable contexts?

2. What are the challenges to Holistic Child Development in the context of slums?

3. To what extent does the existing tuition centres in Chennai slums facilitate Holistic Child Development?

4. What could be a viable model mission tuition centre for children in Chennai slums that would facilitate HCD?

A GRIP

*Significance of Tuition
for HCD in Vulnerable Contexts*

CHAPTER 5

Theological Understanding of Tuition

As we discuss tuition ministry as a mission strategy, we would like to know what God says about tuition. For this we must turn to the Word of God, the Bible. One can see many references in the Bible that portray God's heart for teaching his people in general and children, in particular, in various contexts. Before that let us bear in mind that this book uses the words 'teaching' and 'tuition' synonymously. Because, in addition to teaching, 'tuition' means to point out the activities like counselling, instructing, guiding and such interventions that facilitate holistic development of children.

Teaching viz. Tuition

Generation after generation communities keep up their traditions and customs through teaching their children. Teaching begins in and from home.

"My child, say good morning," a father teaches his child.

"Darling, come on, open your mouth and take this food," a mother teaches her child.

Home teachings include 'dos and don'ts' throughout childhood years and after that too. The most important responsibility of parents is not bread winning but teaching good conduct and character to children. It is also the responsibility of the community to teach children. A Chinese proverb goes like this: "It takes the whole village to develop a child."

Take any civilization in the ancient world, for instance. Religious practices took prominent place in social life. Traditions of rituals, festivals, and ceremonies connected to the deities were taught to following generations by priests diligently. Before writing came into practice, oral form was adopted for religious teachings and every word and passage was memorized by children. It was the responsibility of the king or the chieftain to look after the wellbeing of priests and their families. In some instances, it was not unusual that the priest happened to be the king or vice versa. Melchizedek is an apt example in the Bible (Gen. 16:18-20).

As people of God called to be his priests and prophets in Christ (1 Peter 2:9; Rev.1: 6), it is important to know what God says about teaching. In the Bible, to denote 'teaching' two words are used in the Hebrew language of the Old Testament. One is *yara* meaning 'to point out' and another is *lamad* meaning 'to goad'. In the New Testament, four Greek words are used. They are *didasko* meaning 'to teach', *katecheo* meaning 'to instruct systematically', *paideuo* meaning 'to instruct or train' and *noutheteo* meaning 'to correct, counsel'. Interestingly the meaning of *logos* in the word *theology* is found to be 'teaching'.

The meaning of tuition is generally rendered as 'teaching and instruction'. It could also be 'nurturing the process of development.' The Latin root word *tuitio* means 'guard or guardianship'. A quote from Galatians 3: 23-25 can make it clearer: "Before the faith came, we were held prisoners by the law, locked up until faith should be revealed. So the law was put 'in charge to lead' us to Christ that we might be justified by faith. Now that faith has come, we are no longer under the supervision of the law." The Law of God was the **tutor** until Jesus Christ. Now by faith we have the Holy Spirit as our **tutor**.

God has given humanity the responsibility of teaching and being taught. Through the Bible we find instances of God's priority to teach/instruct his people right from the creation of the world (Gen. 3:16-17, 6:13-21, 9:1-7; Exod. 20:1-17; Deut. 6:1-25). Teaching and learning were not limited to any particular sect of society. Jesus in his great commission commands that all of his teachings be taught to all nations (Mat. 28:18-20).

Contexts of Teaching viz. Tuition in OT

In the Bible, God is known as the tutor who teaches his ways to his people. Ps. 32:8 establishes the tutorship of God. "I will *instruct* you and *teach* you in the way which you shall go: I will *guide* you with my eye." Isa. 48:17 says God is the tutor of his people: "This is what the LORD says- your redeemer, the Holy One of Israel: 'I am the LORD your God, who *teaches* you what is best for you, who *directs* you in the way you should go.'"

God entrusts Moses with tutorship of teaching the people of Israel God's precepts for spiritual matters and social life. "And you shall *teach* them ordinances and laws, and shall *show* them the way they must walk, and the work they must do" (Exod. 18:20). Moses was the tutor who brought the teachings of God to the people. In this sense, all the prophets accomplished their role of tutorship by conveying messages of God by teaching, instructing and guiding the people. "In the past God spoke to our forefathers through the prophets at many times and in various ways" (Heb. 1:1).

God exhorts parents to teach children and the teaching is expected to move on to next generations. Deut. 6:7 reads, "Impress them on your children." God rejects defiled teaching. Mic. 3:11 says, "Her (People of Israel) leaders judge for a bribe, her priests teach for a price, and her prophets tell fortunes for money." God wants to teach children himself. Isa. 54:13 says, "All your children will be taught by the LORD, and great will be your children's peace."

God teaches skills like agriculture and farming. Isa. 28:24-26 says, "When a farmer plows for planting... His God instructs him and *teaches* him the right way." God purported that his people Israel would teach God's precepts of redemption to all nations. Isa. 49:6 says, "I will make you as light for the nations that my salvation may reach to the ends of the earth."

During the period of Diaspora, Jews maintained synagogues for worship as well as for teaching. 'Synagogue' has its root in the Greek word *synagoge* meaning 'leading or bringing together'. It goes well with the meaning of "Tuition"-teaching, training, guiding, etc. Vimala Paulus states, "Wherever Jews lived, synagogues appeared. Pupils learnt reading, writing and arithmetic in the synagogue." It was in the year 64 B.C. when the high priest Joshua ben Gamala made schooling compulsory. Children from age six were to go to the House of Book and children above the age of ten to the House of Study.

Contexts of Teaching viz. Tuition in NT

At the time of the gospels, Jewish children, up to the age five, were taught by the father in the family. After that the boys were sent to synagogue-schools to be taught the Torah. The Hebrew word *Torah* renders the meaning of 'instruction' or 'guidance'. Children sat in groups of twenty five. Extra teachers were appointed if necessary. It was also the responsibility of the father to train boys in a skill and trade for income generation. Girls were trained by the mothers at home in the laws of the Torah in connection to home making, worship, behaviour, culture, music and dance.

Jesus Christ came as a teacher tutoring his hearers on truths of the Kingdom of God. He was called a *rabbi*, a Hebrew word for teacher (Jn 20:16; Mt. 26:49). Matthew recording about Jesus' teaching ministry writes, "He opened his mouth, and *taught* them." (Mt. 5:2) Mark narrates about the helplessness of people and Jesus' teaching with compassion. Mark writes, "And Jesus when he came out, saw much people, and was moved with compassion toward them, because they were as sheep not having shepherd; and he began to teach them many things" (Mk. 6:34). Jesus employed stories for his teaching that his audience of ordinary backgrounds found easy to take in.

Jesus taught in various environmental settings. He taught by the lake (Mk 4:1), synagogues were also used by Jesus for teaching (Lk. 4:15), and houses were places of teaching at times (Mk 3:20). Matthew gives an account of Jesus' teaching in the midst of fields (Mt. 2:1). Mountainsides formed a favourable place for Jesus to teach (Mt. 5:1-2). Jesus was teaching at the temple often towards the end of his ministry (Lk. 20:1, Jn 10:22).

There were children among the people whom Jesus taught. On one occasion Matthew calculates the crowd to be the tune of five thousand besides women and children (Mt. 14:21). At another instance Jesus took a child from among the crowd to teach his disciples (Lk. 9:47).

The Holy Spirit, being the Counsellor, employs teaching for keeping the followers of Jesus Christ in the teachings of Jesus Christ (Jn 14:26). C. Fred Dickason states, "The Holy Spirit is the sovereign, most wise and ultimate teacher of spiritual truth."

Paul advises the church in Ephesus to teach one another through songs and music. "Speak to one another with psalms, hymns and spiritual songs" (Eph. 5: 19). Paul exhorts Timothy, "These things command and *teach*" (1Tim. 4:11).

God-the Father, the Son and the Holy Spirit is still *teaching* and *training* through the Word. All are responsible to pass on what one knows to another through the process of teaching. For in the redemptive plan of God, family and covenant community of Israel in Old Testament and the Church in New Testament are to involve in teaching.

Jesus' Holistic Teaching

Jesus is known as a teacher. He taught the truth with authority (Mt. 7:28-29). Jesus' way of teaching was simple, practical and holistic. Many world leaders have testified to the power of Jesus' teachings which they have followed in their lives.

Spiritual Dimension

Jesus taught that God is Spirit (Jn 4:24). He focused his teaching principally to explain the nature of God and his Kingdom and the Way of restoring an eternal relationship with God. Jesus taught about spiritual truths of worship (Jn 4:24), prayer (Mt. 6:5-15), fasting (Mt. 6:16-18), repentance (Lk. 13:1-9), forgiveness of sins (Mk 2:5-11), purity in heart (Mk 7:1-23), inheriting eternal life (Lk. 10:25-28), the Holy Spirit (Lk. 11:13; Jn 15:26-16:15; Acts 1:8), faith (Mt. 17:20), fellowship with God (Jn 14:23), and judgement (Mt. 25:31-46).

Physical Dimension

Jesus included physical dimension of human development in his teaching. He taught on the importance of food. On two occasions Jesus provided food to the hungry crowd of five thousand (Jn 6:1-10), and four thousand (Mk 8:1-9). According to Mark, Jesus said, "This crowd is breaking my heart. They have stuck with me three days, and now they have nothing to eat. If I send them home hungry, they'll faint along the way- some of them have come a long distance" (Mk 8:2-3 The Message). At another instance Jesus defended his disciples, who were hungry, eating wheat grains on Sabbath (Mt. 12:1-8). He taught that physical needs must be met when it is required.

Jesus healed the sick and the lame (Mt. 15:26-31). Through his healing ministry Jesus taught that physical development is necessary for one's progressive social living. He set aside time to go for rest for rejuvenating physical strength. Mark records, "Jesus said, 'Come off by yourselves; let's take a break and get a little rest.'

For there was constant coming and going. They didn't even have time to eat" (Mk 6:31 The Message).

Cognitive Dimension

The teachings of Jesus were also purported to impart cognitive development. Jesus asked questions in order to make his listeners reason out and respond. Jesus used the method of questions and answers to start a conversation and drive home his teachings to his hearers.

When he was twelve years old, Jesus taught the Jewish teachers through debate (Lk. 2:46). Jesus affirmed that reading through the Scriptures leads to understanding his mission (Jn 5:39). He expected the audience to understand scriptures and respond intellectually. Jesus refers to working out an estimation of expenses for building a tower when he taught about discipleship (Lk. 14:28).

Social Dimension

Jesus taught to lead a life of happiness, contentment and social harmony. His parables mostly draw insights from day to day situations of social life. His parables are found referring to various aspects of business, administration, family, affluence, poverty, friendship, celebrations, trades, travel, occupation and banking (Mt. 13:1-50; 18:23-35; 20:1-16; 22:1-14; 25:1-30, Lk. 10:30-37; 12:16-21; 14:28-35; 15; 18:1-8; 16:1-8; 19-31). Ecological aspects of social sphere of human life also found place in his teachings. The teachings of Jesus were meant for social transformation which is more than mere personal or individual benefits. Though Jesus belonged to the Jewish culture, his teaching was universal irrespective of the diverse cultural practices of communities in the world.

It is, henceforth, very clear that tutoring is as divine and spiritual as worship is. It is to be carried out in all godliness and devotion. Tuition is not to be limited to academic interest only. They have a preset goal of preparing children to get through exams. But in the mission of God, tuition is meant to care for every aspect of a child's development. Nothing less and nothing more!

A Christian tutor needs to have the conviction of God's call to serve children. Even without any specific academic qualification the tutor can provide tuition by way of regular visits, counselling, giving time to listen, encouraging in times of despair, strengthening through cheering words, and imparting optimistic attitude. All that is required is a heart that reflects the heart of God for children. The unshakable conviction that it is God's mandate to care for children at risk is the only motivating force that drives the tutor to do the best.

CHAPTER 6

HCD of Children at Risk in the Bible

The Bible talks about children who lived in a particular time and context of world history. They are not myths; nor are they epics. They are real life stories. Learning about vulnerable life situations of those children make us conscious about children at risk today. The ways God intervened in the lives of such children show the need of local churches to do their best for the children at risk nearby.

Childhood of Jesus

The childhood of Jesus was not trouble free. Like many children in Chennai slums, Jesus went through highly vulnerable situations as a child. Birth of Jesus, family's economic status, migration to Egypt and the town of Nazareth were some of the factors that made the childhood of Jesus vulnerable. Being tutored by his parents and schooling could be seen as some of the factors that contributed to his holistic development.

Atypical Birth

Mary getting pregnant before her marriage to Joseph is a profoundly serious issue. Besides raising suspicions, it could have even cost Mary her life by way of death at the hands of the Jewish authorities since a sexual relationship was not permitted before all the three stages of Jewish wedding process were completed, the three stages being agreement, announcement and wedding. The revelation from God was not given to all but Mary and Joseph only (Lk. 2:30; Mt. 1:20). Sanjiv Ailawadi states that the birth of the Son of God was perceived as a social stigma.

Poor Family

Jesus was born in an artisan's family, his father Joseph being a village carpenter (Mt. 13:55). J.C. Ryle points out that the family of Jesus lived in poverty. John MacArthur endorses this, commenting on Lk. 2:24 that Joseph and Mary were so poor that they could afford only a pair of doves or pigeons according to the law stated in Lev. 12:8. David Brown states that the poor status of Jesus' parents can be understood from the sacrifices they were able to offer, 'a pair of doves or two young pigeons.'

Migration Risks

The Gospel of Luke tells us that Joseph and Mary travelled 90 miles from Nazareth to Bethlehem for census enrolment. Again, when Jesus was about two years old, Joseph and Mary had to flee to Egypt on account of King Herod's order to execute children below two years in Bethlehem (Mt. 2:16-21). In Egypt they lived as refugees with Joseph working as a labourer. Jesudason Baskar Jeyaraj views this as a political dimension that causes vulnerability of children. Roy B. Zuck observes that there were frequent travels in the first few years of childhood of Jesus with risks of unsafe mode of travelling.

Complex Society of Nazareth

Jesus grew up as a boy in the Galilean town called Nazareth. Family life here was not comfortable with houses made only with mud bricks and a distinct lack of privacy. Nazareth was reputed for immorality and ungodliness. Thomas Manjaly renders a comprehensive picture of life in Nazareth. He states, "Galilee was 'geographically and theologically' distant from, and 'religiously' despised by Jerusalem (Galilee of the Gentiles—Mt. 4:15; Isa. 9:1), 'socially' isolated by Samaria, 'politically' threatened by its neighbours and 'economically' marginalized, largely peasant population, by Romans." The description of Nazareth is found to be tantamount to Chennai slums. Hence, we deduce that the place of his childhood posed challenges to the holistic development of child Jesus.

Traditional Tutoring

It is observed that amidst vulnerable childhood situations, the holistic development of child Jesus was facilitated through tutoring by parents and teachers. The following sections study some of the elements related to the significance of tuition in nurturing HCD of Jesus.

Spiritual Nurture by Parents

Joseph and Mary were God-fearing parents who were the adherents of Jewish religious customs as given in the law (Lk. 2:22-24). They regularly went to the temple in Jerusalem every year to celebrate the festival of Passover and Jesus was also taken with them when he was twelve years old (Lk. 2:41). Jesus grew up under godly parents.

Education

Zuck opines that Jesus was taught in 'home-school' by parents and at 'synagogue school' by teachers at the age of six. The fact that Jewish children are sent to school when they are six years old is complemented by Vimala Paulus. Dan Brewster states that child Jesus learnt from Jewish rabbis like any other child in Nazareth, as well as through watching, observing and listening. Schooling experience was necessary for cognitive development of child Jesus.

Livelihood

In Jewish society, it is the responsibility of the father to teach his son the family trade when the son turns fifteen. Jesus learnt carpentry from Joseph, his earthly father.

Tutoring and Spiritual Development

Samuel—Child among Wicked Priests

The story of Samuel illustrates how Samuel in his childhood developed spiritually in spite of challenges prevailing both in his family and in the house of the Lord in Shiloh. Some of the challenging factors as well as favourable factors for the spiritual development of child Samuel are discussed here.

Disgraceful Impact of Polygamy

Michael Eaton affirms the cultural dimension of gaining social status corresponding to the number of children a woman has. Harry Mowvley comments that since Israelites had no hope of life after death children were considered as bearers of family name for the next generation. Such convictions gave way for second marriage and surrogacy and naturally these practices caused conflicts in family relationships. The Bible informs that Peninnah, the other wife of Elkana, ill-treated Hannah (1Sam. 1:6). It can be inferred that Samuel, born to Hannah, also experienced unloving treatment from Peninnah. Children can be affected by the disputes and indifferences prevailing in polygamous families. The early childhood of Samuel should have been affected by unhealthy relationships in the family.

Vulnerable Situation of Shiloh

F.B. Meyer suggests that Samuel was taken to Shiloh at the age of three. The times of his coming into the service of the Tabernacle were not favourable to the spiritual formation and development of the child Samuel. Michael Eaton points out that there was sin in the sanctuary. K.G. Jose expounds that the children of Eli were agents of evil.

Tutoring Samuel for Spiritual Development

Samuel was born into a God-fearing family. Matthew Henry comments that Elkanah, Samuel's father continued his annual visits to the Lord's house despite intra-family disputes. Hannah, the mother of Samuel, was a godly woman. She was a woman of prayer and faith (1 Sam. 1:10, 2:1-10). F.B. Meyer further states that the life of a mother influences children. Hannah was the first tutor to young Samuel. Secondly, Eli was the tutor to Samuel, teaching the child God's laws pertaining to the service of a priest. Samuel developed under the tutorship of both Hannah and Eli.

A direct contact and communication of God himself with the child is also recorded in the Bible (1Sam. 3). God also plays the role of tutor. MacArthur refers to the Jewish historian Flavius Josephus as predicting the age of Samuel to be twelve when he had an encounter with God.

Timothy—Child of Mixed Marriage

Timothy lived in Lystra, a Galatian town and a Roman colony. His father was Greek and his mother was Jewish (Acts 16:1). Peter Wagner points out that both Timothy and his mother Eunice became Christians during Paul's first mission. MacArthur suggests that Timothy should have been in his late teens or early twenties when Paul met him and that it is likely that his father was no more. The churches nearby gave a good report about Timothy. Timothy is found to have had developed to be a church leader.

The following sections discuss some of the challenges child Timothy encountered with respect to his development in family and society.

Family Environment

In the Greco-Roman culture, the father had the sole legal authority to exercise unlimited control over his children and wife. The Life Application Study Bible commenting on Acts 16:1-5 says, "Although Timothy's father apparently was not a Christian, the faithfulness of Timothy's mother and grand-mother prevailed." It can be inferred that the conversion of Eunice and Timothy to Christian faith could have had reactions from the Greek husband/father. Such faith differences among parents could have had a serious impact on the development of the child Timothy.

Mixed Social Identity

Since Timothy was born in a family of mixed marriage, there were problems related to customs and traditions. Timothy had to live among the traditions of both the Greeks and the Jews. Traditions are important to children. F.F. Bruce states that Gentiles would have looked at Timothy as a Jew and Jews would have looked at him as a Gentile. Further, children from such mixed family background were considered as Samaritans by Jews. Living in a mixed family was a challenge to the development of child Timothy from a social perspective.

Health Issue

From 1 Tim. 5:23 it is noted that Timothy had some health issues that had to be cared for. The development of child Timothy should have been challenged by this ailment.

Development Support by Tutelage

For Timothy, the faith tradition of his ancestors was a great advantage. His mother and grandmother were the first tutors for child Timothy (2 Tim. 1:5). Zuck quotes Lucien Coleman as suggesting that Timothy probably had an opportunity of being tutored by a pedagogue, who was a responsible guard and mentor of the child's education. Paul contributed significantly as a mentor in the life of Timothy. We find a tutor in Paul caring for young Timothy.

Tutoring and Physical Development

Ishmael—Abandoned to Die

The narrative of Abraham in the Old Testament explains the stressful and debilitating family circumstances the child Ishmael was born in to. Life Application Study Bible renders that Ishmael was born into a 'tense atmosphere.' Ishmael was in his adolescence, about sixteen years of age when Abraham dispelled Hagar. For a while, child Ishmael had no place to live in. With divine intervention and his mother's nurture, Ishmael developed to be the founder of twelve Arabic tribes known as the Ishmaelites to which Mohammed, founder of Islam, claimed to belong. Ishmael died at the age of 137.

Challenges to the Physical Wellbeing

Adam Clarke explains that Abraham directed Hagar towards a specific location but she missed the direction and got lost in the wilderness. When food ran out, the sorrowing mother was helpless without any possibility of saving her son from death (Gen. 21:15). Clarke recognises the difference between teens and adults; comparatively teens cannot bear more stress and they perspire more, needing more water and their digestive process is faster making them feel hungry soon.

Tutored by Abraham

A comparison of Gen. 16:16 and 17:1 confirms that Ishmael was thirteen years old when God reminded Abraham about the birth of Isaac. Eaton comments, "Abraham became fond of Ishmael and all his hopes have been wrapped up in him. He has been Abraham's only son for more than thirteen years." Ron Lyles and others affirm that Abraham expected all the promises of God to be fulfilled in Ishmael. It can, therefore, be contended that Ishmael developed under the careful tutorship of Abraham. Circumcision of Ishmael confirms that he was taught by Abraham everything pertaining to covenant faith. G.J. Wenham states that Ishmael prayed at the time of trouble. It was probably Abraham who taught child Ishmael to pray. Ishmael learnt from his father to depend on and pray to God for physical needs.

Role of Tutoring Mother

Matthew Henry explaining God's promise for Ishmael, states, "It should engage our care and pains about children and young people, to consider that we know not what great use God has designed them for, and may make of them." It can be observed that Hagar's nurturing Ishmael until she was sent out by Abraham formed his physical growth. At the time of crisis in the desert, Hagar's presence contributed to sustaining the child's confidence and courage. Being supportive to the survival of someone under one's charge is considered as tutelage. Robert Jamieson, A.R. Fausset and David Brown, commenting on Hagar, observe that she played the role of a father to find a wife for Ishmael. Hagar is found tutoring her son by guarding and guiding him to see that her child develops to be a healthy and successful adult (Gen. 21:20-21).

Joash—Child in Political Conspiracy

Joash was the son of Ahaziah the sixth king of Judah (2 Kgs 11:2). Zibiah of Beersheba was his mother (2 Kgs 12:1). He was one year old when his aunt Jehosheba protected him from being killed by his grandmother Athaliah in Jerusalem (2 Chron. 22:10-11). At the very young age of seven, Joash was crowned the king of Judah and reigned for forty years (2 Chron. 24:1).

Ungodly Family Hereditary

Athaliah, the grandmother of Joash was the granddaughter of Omri, the king of Israel (2 Chron. 22:2). Omri was the father of King Ahab of Israel (1 Kgs 16:29). She was the daughter of Jezebel, wicked queen of King Ahab of Israel. Athaliah seems to have inherited all the evil characters of her mother Jezebel who had slain the prophets of God in Israel (1 Kgs 18:13, 19:1).

Loss of Life due to Power crisis

On finding that all her wickedness were coming to an end at the death of her son Ahazia, Athaliah ordered the killing of all her grandsons (2 Chron. 22:10). For the selfish gains of parents, children are victimised. By the brave intervention of his aunt, child Joash and his nurse escaped from the mass killing.

Factors Contributing to Development amidst Crisis

It is observed that Joash's aunt Jehosheba was voluntarily involved in saving the life of the child Joash. Jehosheba was also the wife of the priest Jehoiada (2 Chron. 22:11). It is evident that it was a strategic attempt by a team of brave people to protect the child from any physical harm. A team was at work to nurture the child Joash holistically.

Clarke points out that the place where the child Joash was nurtured was the temple sanctuary since no one had access to enter it. It provided a conducive environment for the holistic development in general and physical development in particular of the child. MacArthur states that the priest Jehoiada was the 'tutor' for the child. The child king Joash could bring out religious changes under the guidance of the tutor priest. Children can be agents of change if they are guided properly. They need to be protected against violence and exploitation.

Tutoring and Cognitive Development

Moses—Educated for Leading a Nation

Childhood challenges

Moses' early childhood was surrounded by dangerous circumstances due to the decree of Pharaoh who misused the river Nile, God's providence and the people of God. This is tantamount to slum scenarios where people in power and authority sell canal banks and open lands to slum families and keep them suppressed.

The identity of Moses was another factor that kept the child at risk. A resemblance could be observed between the name Moses and the names of Egyptian kings Ahmose, Thutmose, and Ramses.

It is evident that the Hebrew child was so named by the Egyptian princess so that the ethnic identity could be concealed.

Timely Intervention by Brave women

Stuart highlights the role of women in saving the life of Moses, one of them being Miriam, his own sister in her childhood. The age of Miriam is assumed to have been between six and twelve years. The other one was the princess of Egypt. By the interference of women of two opposing societies, the life of Moses during his childhood was saved.

Development of Cognitive Skills

Egypt was known for its wisdom and knowledge. Josephus comments that as the prince of Egypt, Moses had access to every opportunity for his development. Philo is said to have written that Moses became an expert in music, geometry, mathematics, arts and sciences. Roger E. Hedlund suggests that Moses was educated in some more skills like athletics, writing, law, medicine, literature, astronomy, and philosophy. Commenting on Acts 7:22, J.A. Alexander writes Moses was *taught* and *instructed* in all knowledge and wisdom. Teaching and instructing are part of tutoring. F.F. Bruce refers to the belief of Hellenistic Jews that Moses was the founder of science and culture of Egyptian civilization. Josephus portrays Moses as a victorious army leader who defeated Ethiopia. Hence, opportunities for development of skills and knowledge made Moses a prominent leader in Egypt and later on in Israel.

Daniel—Top Ranker in Captivity

MacArthur comments that Daniel was possibly in his teens, around 15 years of age when he was taken to Babylon while A.R. Millard maintains that Daniel was twelve or thirteen years old. However, it can be ascertained that Daniel was in his late childhood or in early adolescence.

An Account of Challenges

When Jerusalem was captured in 605 B.C.by Nebuchadnezzar, young men and women were taken captive to Babylon to be trained for government services (Dan. 1:4). Daniel and his three friends were among the hostages. Life in exile was the first and foremost challenge for the four young Jews.

They were to forego their own culture and embrace Babylonian life style. Their Jewish names were changed into Babylonian names (Dan. 1:6-7). These pagan names carried meanings in honour of pagan deities 'Baal' and 'Arku'. Vernon McGee sees the risk of these preadolescent boys being brainwashed to become Babylonians in every aspect of their life. It is probable that Daniel was turned to be a eunuch.

Raising to honour by tuition

From the way Daniel employs two languages to write the book of Daniel in the Old Testament, it is evident that he had mastered both Hebrew and Aramaic, the common language of Babylon. It is also possible that Daniel studied the Babylonian official language of Chaldean and the literary language of Akkadian that derived its writing system from the Sumerian language. In the Old Testament, the word 'literature' appears only in the book of Daniel. Such cognitive skill in languages imparted through the royal tuition enabled Daniel to rise to the level of the Governor of the province (Dan. 2:48). He served in the governments of three consecutive emperors - Nebuchadnezzar, Belshazzar and Darius.

Tutoring and Social Development

Jephthah—From Discrimination to Recognition

The episode of Jephthah is found in Judg. 11:1-12:7. His father was Gilead and his mother was not the legal wife of his father (Judg.11:1). 'Concubine' and 'harlot' are the two words used in the New International Bible Dictionary for his mother. She was a Canaanite woman. Jephthah later became the judge of Israel for six years.

Vulnerability due to family background

The profession of Jephthah's mother as a prostitute might have been a problem for Jephthah in his social life. Samapika Mohapatra maintains that the occupation of parents has a predominant influence on the development of children. Sakhi Athyal refers to Erik Erikson who suggests that children develop a sense of shame, doubt and guilt in their early childhood. Jephthah's step brothers despised him because he was born to an illegitimate mother. Zuck affirms that children illegitimately born are emotionally offended as they grow. He comments, "Jephthah, also illegitimately born because his mother was a prostitute, experienced conflict with his half brothers, who drove him out of town." Socially neglected and deprived due to the fault of his parents, Jephthah's childhood was a time of struggle with respect to social development.

Strengths of Jephthah

Commenting on Jephthah, Warren Wiersbe states that he developed to be a man of faith and courage knowing the scriptures. When Jephthah was ill treated by his step brothers he fled to live in the vicinity of Tob, the Aramaean city (Judg. 11:3). Aramaeans were known for their literary excellence with respect to business and administration. There he learnt to be an able diplomatic organiser with a band of men following him. Under Jephthah's commandership these bandits were earning their livelihood by looting travellers and settlements. Robert Jamieson and others observe that it was a normal profession. They write, "It is not deemed dishonourable when the expeditions are directed against those out of his tribe or nation." P.R. Ackroyd and others assert that Jephthah developed his capacity in military operations at Tob. It can be contended that Jephthah socially developed to be a successful military commander under an unknown tutelage.

Esther-Queen from Minority Society

Young Girl

Esther was taken to the palace when she was in a marriageable age. Luis Bush alludes that Esther was probably in her later teens when she was taken into the Persian palace. Hadassah, meaning 'Myrtle,' was her Jewish name and Esther is Persian meaning 'Star'; she lived during the time of King Xerxes of Persia in 486 B.C. The story of Esther shows how an orphaned girl child tutored by her cousin brother reached the heights of prominent social life.

Vulnerable Family situation

Esther's parents could have been killed by the army of Nebuchadnezzar, making her an orphan. She, being an orphan, was taken care of by her cousin Mordecai (Es. 2:7).

Vulnerable Social situation

It is a society with male dominating culture that keeps women marginalised and oppressed. In that case, the fate of young girls who were not chosen by the King Xerxes should have been questionable. MacArthur writes, commenting on Esth. 3:4, "It seems evident from Haman's fury and attempted genocide, that there were strong anti-Semitic attitudes in Shushan, which seems to explain Mordecai's reluctance to reveal his true ethnic background." Jews were living as a minority in Persia. The way Jews were socially discriminated against could be understood from Mordecai's advice to Esther not to reveal her social identity as a Jew when she was taken into the palace (Es. 2:10).

Vulnerable Political Situation

Jews were a minority and a powerless community living in the foreign country of Persia. Joyce G. Baldwin comments, "Life in Persia under the rule of King Xerxes was oppressive for minority groups like the Jews and, according to the writer of Esther, perilous."

Factors enabling Esther to overcome Challenges

First, it was the role of Mordecai that played the vital part in the development of Esther from childhood. He was so concerned about her development that when Esther was taken into the palace, Mordecai was keen on monitoring her welfare (Es. 2:11). Second, it was the time when synagogues were founded during Jews' Babylonian captivity. The synagogues were the places of elementary education of children. It is worth noting the tradition of a Great Synagogue of Persian period in which Mordecai was a member. Diligent tutoring in childhood pays well in later times of life. Third, the caretaker in the palace was willing to extend all necessary support to Esther. It is, hence, observed that a child in a deprived state can be successful with the care and support of compassionate adults.

We see that children in Bible were also going through vulnerable situations. The reasons for vulnerability arise from family circumstances, social practices and political situations. All these situations challenge a child's development altogether. But God immediately intervenes. He uses men and women and even children sometimes to fulfil his purpose of developing a child at risk holistically.

That is precisely what missionaries did when they came to Tamil Nadu with the gospel of Jesus Christ. When they saw children in highly vulnerable environments, they did not keep silent. They did everything in their means to help them. Most of them laid down their life for the emancipation of the downtrodden communities and for the development of their children. The times we live in requires our looking back to the works of missionaries for children's development and follow their footsteps, in relevance to present context.

CHAPTER 7

Mission Initiatives for HCD of Children at Risk

The dawn of 19th century saw the flourishing of missionary societies abroad. It was a century of missionaries pouring in British India. They came to preach the gospel, gather believers as churches and develop local leaders. In the pursuit of obeying the Great Commission of Jesus Christ, no time was lost, on the way, by missionaries in availing every opportunity to serve 'Children...for their health...for their education and for their whole development.' While the imperialistic bureaucrats of the British were working towards longevity of colonial governance, missionaries were committed to the Kingdom of God in line with the Nazareth manifesto of Jesus Christ: "The Spirit of the Lord is on me, because he has anointed me to preach good news to the poor. He has sent me to proclaim freedom for the prisoners and recovery of sight for the blind, to release the oppressed, to proclaim the year of the Lord's favour" (Luke 4:18-19). Almost all over Tamil Nadu mission boarding homes and schools were opened by missions particularly for children of oppressed communities. This led to a great harvest in transformation of Tamil society at large through multiplying of churches and revolutionary reformation among Hindus.

When we were young children, our parents used to say, "If you don't behave yourselves and get good marks in exams then we will put you in boarding homes. That is the place to learn life properly." Every time we approached our father for signing in the progress cards we heard this.

In the turn of 20th century, boarding homes were there to cater to the need of children from poverty stricken families, particularly from Christian families. Those were times when people were under heavy suppression in the name of caste hierarchy. Mission boarding homes acted as ladders of HCD for the children of the most disadvantaged families with Christian care given by missionaries for the formation of their whole personality. This made it possible for a life of dignity as they could find employments in schools, hospitals, government departments, companies and factories.

Let me narrate a real story. About a decade ago I met a man in his sixties. He told me that he was retired from Bank services and well settled. On hearing about my involvement in mission among children through tuition centres in Odisha, he began to recollect his childhood experiences in a children's home in the town of Sirkali, near Thanjavur in Tamil Nadu.

He said, "My father died when I was studying in 5th class. I was sent to this home in Sirkali run by Tamil Evangelical Lutheran Mission. Every day children had to get up by 5 in the morning and sit for studies after prayer. Rice porridge was given as breakfast in measures according to class of study. Three cups for elementary school children and five cups for high school children. In spite of such bottlenecks I am what I am only because of the boarding home and school." Thousands of such beneficiaries of mission boarding homes can be identified today all over Tamil Nadu.

Reminiscence of Distresses

From the view point of a missionary, life of out-castes was utterly hopeless. The world view was that it was their fate. No one could help. They reap in this birth what they sowed in the previous birth. The distressful life of outcastes was preordained by their god. It was beyond human intervention. They were made to believe that serving the Brahmins and other high caste people could release them from curse in their next birth. Until then, they were to live it.

Boys were sold as child labours to drama companies and other industries. Girl children were given away to temples as 'dancing girls.' Child sacrifices were quite common. Parents were willing to sacrifice their new born children under the wheels of temple chariots during festivals as fulfilment of their vows. In remote rural areas, child trafficking and slavery were in practice. Female infanticides were quite common among ignorant rural communities. It is quite moving to note that young girls and women of lower caste of Nadars were not allowed to wear upper cloth. Families with children migrated out of villages as bonded labours to work in tea estates, brick chambers and rice mills.

Local sorcery and soothsayers were consulted to fix the time of child birth. Legs of mother were tied in order to prevent child birth before the auspicious time. Several unborn infants and mothers died unscrupulously due to this cruel practice. Child marriage was rampant. Child widows were blamed for the death of their husbands. Children died in numbers due to acute famines. Spread of diseases like Cholera and Plague killed thousands of children as there were no medical remedies available. Children were affected to the level of being sold due to consecutive cyclones, famine and killer deceases. Missionaries believed that not doing anything about it was sin against a holy and loving God.

Schools run by missionaries were affected due to caste discriminations. Dominant caste people protested not to admit children from Dalit families. Schools were closed for years. Children could not continue education because of such social evils of those times. Even in the 20th century, Dalit children were not allowed to wear foot wear by the dominant caste people who were the job providers for Dalits. In all circumstances, missionaries won the day by standing firmly on the truth of the gospel and serving children tirelessly.

Mission Boarding Homes

In children's homes, all the aspects of a child's development were taken care of. Each activity was planned and carried out meticulously by committed Christian staff that led to HCD. Prayers, Sunday school, Bible classes and Sunday church worship services contributed to the **spiritual development** of children in the homes. Nutritious meals, medical care, playground activities, garden works, physical exercises, scheduled duties of cleaning and washing took care of both **physical and social development**. Morning and evening study time to complete school homework and compulsory schooling facilitated **cognitive development**. Loving care and affectionate counselling by teachers, staff, evangelists, pastors and church congregation helped the children for **social development**. Even after many years a person who grew up in a boarding home can pinpoint the name of the child care staff or teacher or someone who gave counselling in times of need. Above all, exemplary witnessing live models of Christians around the children were very effective in the formation of Christ-like citizens.

Lutheran Mission

The first Protestant missionary Bartholomaus Ziegenbalg was from a German Lutheran background. Sent by the King of Denmark under Royal Danish Mission he arrived in Tranquebar, Tamil Nadu along with co-missionary Henrich Pluetschau in 1706. On seeing the prevalence of extreme poverty he began to nurture children by opening boarding homes. He persevered in his social obligations to poor children despite opposition from the mission board in Denmark. It so happened that when he came to know about the impending justice to a widow and her children, he wrote an appeal to the Danish Governor without delay. This made the Governor behave ruthlessly by ordering the imprisonment of Ziegenbalg. Finally, Ziegenbalg won the case and the widow received their property back from her husband's relatives. He was quite particular about tutoring Tamil children in the Word of God.

In the second half of 18th century a German Lutheran missionary, C.F. Schwartz arrived in Tranquebar. Wars broke out between the British and the French for expanding their business boundaries. Due to this, the French Roman Catholic people persecuted families of Protestant faith. Many families found refuge in Tranquebar and C.F. Schwartz provided shelter and employment for parents and education for children. He opened an orphanage in Thiruchirappalli town for the children who lost their parents in a public fire accident. Later on, Schwartz was inducted by the mission of Society for Propagation of Christian Knowledge (SPCK). A boarding home was opened in Tanjore where the famous Tamil Christian poet Vedanayagam Sastriyar (1774-1864) grew up under the care of Schwartz.

In the following years, Lutheran Mission opened boarding homes for girls in Porayar, Mayavaram and Sirkazhi in Tanjore region and Pandur near Chennai.

Women missionaries were trained in running boarding homes. More boarding homes were started in the first decades of 20th century in Sathur, Kamuthi and Usilampatti of Madurai region for boys and girls. A school and a boarding home for visually challenged children were founded in Tiruppathur in Ramnad region. These children apprenticed in cottage industry of hand loom and the products brought in funds to run the home. Paul Sandegren, a Swedish Missionary of Lutheran tradition, is one of the heroes of HCD in the first half of the twentieth century in Tamil Nadu. He provided holistic care to rural children in homes. It is estimated that in a period of twenty years, 1952-72, about 30,000 children were benefited.

Arcot Lutheran Church (ALC) was founded by the Danish Mission Society (DMS). In the year 1864, DMS established its station in Cuddalore district of Tamil Nadu. Schools and Boarding Homes were established in Cuddalore, Thiruvannamali and Thirkoilur districts from 1893 onwards. In 1900 an industrial school was opened, and in 1921 an orphanage was started.

Missouri Lutheran Evangelical India Mission (MLEIM), the mother mission of present India Evangelical Lutheran Church (IELC), founded schools in the early 20th century in the most backward parts of Tamil Nadu. One account of Sunday Schools and Vacation Bible Schools conducted by IELC in 1965-72 states that children from Hindu and Muslim families were attending the classes. They opened children's homes for girls in schools and vocational training. Later homes for boys were started.

SPCK Mission

The foremost objective of SPCK was the development of poor children through education. Dark clouds of war were hovering over the days of missionary John Philip Fabricius when he arrived at Madras in 1742 under the patronage of SPCK. At the time of his arrival in Madras, there was a church that was used as school and a Mission house that served as a boarding home as well. In 1746-48, French army took over St. George Fort of English East India Company. Fabricius had to take refuge, along with 12 orphans, in Pulicut, a Danish settlement on the seashore north of Madras, two times. A school was started in Pulicut where children were taught Tamil and Portuguese. SPCK opened an asylum for girls in Madras in the year 1787. Another asylum for boys was opened in 1789.

Methodist Mission

According to Methodist Mission, individual conversion and social reformation were the two-sided outcome expected from missionary work. One of the earliest boarding homes in Madras was the one in Rayapetta built by the Methodist Mission in 1850 that housed about 150 girls to continue their schooling. William Goudie joined them who is remembered for his inspiring work to uplift the poor in the district of Thiruvallur about 40 kms West of Chennai. Goudie in one of his letters in 1891 writes about children who spent their childhood starving and working hard for the family by collecting firewood, cow-dung and looking after sheep and goats from the morning. He was well aware that children are vulnerable to lose character due to lifelong oppression and hunger. What he said in 1898 still holds good today: "The love which we preach must take form in service… what more effective preaching than this, to defend the poor and the fatherless, to see that such as are in need and necessarily have right; to deliver the out-caste and poor, and save them from the hand of the ungodly... this is the love of God." He believed in unconditional service to poor irrespective of their response to the gospel. After his return from furlough, Goudie renovated a boarding home in Ikkadu with a capacity of 100 children. Boys were accommodated in 'Southern Cross Home,' sponsored by Methodists in Melbourne and girls in 'Burnham Home.'

In 1889, Goudie sowed the seed for medical ministry in Ikkadu. In 1894, he built a hospital there. A note in the biographical book *William Goudie* by V. Daniel Mohanraj reveals that about 34,000 people visited the hospital in a year. With Ikkadu hospital as centre, medical ministry was expanded in five more places. When the epidemic of Cholera attacked villagers, this hospital saved many lives.

Church Missionary Society (CMS)

CMS missionary Charles T.E. Rhenius came to Madras in 1814. The very next year he started a school where 46 boys enrolled. Sometimes he gave jobs to men so that they could feed the children in their families. Rhenius taught that laziness and casteism were two evils believers must get rid of. He was very particular about personal evangelism that often he talked to young boys and responded to their arguments. In 1820, Rhenius left Madras for Palamkottai in South Tamil Nadu. There was a seminary in the town of Tinnaveli where young boys from local churches were trained for evangelistic work. CMS took up running the seminary under the supervision of Rhenius. A seminary for women was established in 1823, the second in its kind India. 23 girls enrolled in the seminary. There were thirteen schools in the villages surrounding Tinnaveli and the number of students was 411. CMS bought lands for Christian families who were persecuted by others. That was how many Christian villages that exist even today were created. During Cholera epidemic and famine in 1830s CMS served 200-300 families both Christians and others sparingly.

Church of Scotland Mission

Even today the name Alexander Silver echoes around the city of Arakkonam, 100 kms west of Chennai, for his ardent service in the years 1910-1923, for the emancipation of children of Dalits. Under the Church of Scotland Mission, Silver gave himself fully in the works of evangelism, schools, boarding homes and medical services in villages. The landlords of high caste communities vehemently opposed conversions of Dalits. They could not tolerate seeing the development the Christian faith and life brought in the lives of the Dalit families and children. They, therefore, denied water from the village well for the Christians. No job was offered to them. Their hut houses were set on fire. They were beaten cruelly. In later years the situations changed as children began to develop through the mission schools and homes. In 1929, there were 27 students from villages in the boarding home. In addition to school, they were trained in cultivation, weaving, mat making and construction works.

Baptist Mission

Strict Baptist Mission arrived in Tamil Nadu in about 1900. On finding children in vulnerable situations, boarding homes were opened in the towns of Namakkal and Koilpatti. Another mission known as Cylone India General Mission of Baptist Convictions worked among villages in Coimbatore. It had boarding homes in Andhiyur and Gobichettipalayam.

Health Care Services

In 1794, Schwartz saved hundreds of children in schools and villages of Southern Tamil Nadu from smallpox by introducing vaccination. Danish Mission Society founded hospitals in Thirukoilur and Virudachalamin 1911 and 1925 respectively. When John Scudder working with Arcot Mission founded a hospital in Kanyakumari District in 1819, London Missionary Society and Church Missionary Society came up to start medical ministry in Tamil Nadu. Ida Scudder qualified herself as doctor and founded the Christian Medical College and Hospital in Vellore in 1917 for the benefit of the poor and Paul Brand provided medical care to the tribals of Kolli hills. In 1911, a clinic was operated by the Strict Baptist Mission for the benefit of slum dwellers in Chennai.

Christian Child Development Organizations

After the Second World War, **World Vision (WV)** was founded in 1950. The cry of founder Pierce, a pastor and missionary to China was, "Let my heart be broken with the things that break the heart of God." This is an International organization for relief and development with special attention of serving children at risk. Homes that were sponsored by WV are no longer in operation in India. WV networks with government departments for sustainable growth of communities focussing on children. **Kinder not hilfe (KNH)**, a German based Christian child care organization, had been active in India since 1959. It worked among child labours and street children in megacities like Chennai. About 92,680 children have received help from KNH through 325 projects in India. Supported by **Red een Kind (REK)** of Netherlands, thousands of Children were cared for HCD by about 22 Christian organizations like Bethel Agricultural Fellowship in Tamil Nadu in the second half of the twentieth century. Children were nurtured in homes and schools as well. Today homes have been closed. A project by the name Child Centred Community Development has been undertaken by REK from the beginning of 21st century. **Christian Mission Service (CMS)** founded in 1957 ran homes, day care centres and vocational training programs in Tamil Nadu and other states of India. CMS is supported by donors from Germany and Switzerland. These homes are kept under close scrutiny of the government.

Every child care project by Christian organizations is under the scanner of government with an eye on foreign fund flows. Moreover, boarding homes are out of context these days. Comparing to the times of foreign missionaries, life situations of disadvantaged communities today are far better than they were before. Nonetheless, there is a long way to go to see the end of injustice caused to children of outcastes. The era of indigenous missions began with Indian Mission Society (IMS) founded in 1903, followed by National Missionary Society (NMS) in 1905. IMS sent missionaries to Dornakal in Andhra where schools for downtrodden outcastes children were started, that brought social liberation and transformation. But why such educational mission efforts were completely neglected by indigenous missions of Independent India is the question that remains to be answered.

CHAPTER 8

Childhood of Great Christians

All of us can recollect how we developed holistically in our childhood days and who our informal tutors were who contributed to our holistic development. Likewise, childhood stories of great Christian achievers are full of such tutelage for their holistic development. These Christian stalwarts grew up amidst vulnerable life situations. Yet, they received God-sent assistance through their own family or friends or other benefactors like teachers, missionaries and pastors. Some of them are discussed below:

Martin Luther

The great leader of Church Reformation, Martin Luther was born on 10th November 1483, in Eisleben, Germany, in a poor family. His parents Hans Luther and Margaret hailed from a working class of peasant community. His mother used to collect firewood in the forest and carried it home on her back. Six months after Martin was born, his father went to Mansfield to work as a miner in Copper mines. Parents were his first tutors in life. Martin learned life values of honesty, hard work, fear of God, prayer, contentment, honour of education, and joy of music and singing. His parents were very particular about Martin's education that his father carried him to school on his shoulders. Martin was proud of his father when he was elected to be a member of the Mansfield City Council.

At the age of seven, Martin was admitted into a school where students were only allowed to speak in Latin. Those who disobeyed would be severely punished. Subjects were memorized since there were no printed books available. There were no religious teachings in school. Church was the place where Martin enjoyed music and singing. He grew to be a talented violinist. A foundation was laid here that gave fruits of several songs composed by Martin on Christian faith and life.

In 1497, Luther sent his son to a school in Magdeburg that was run by Brethren of the Common Life. It was here that Martin came to know about living as a monk. In the next year, he was sent to continue his education in another city, Eisenach. He stayed in one of his relatives' homes. Martin used his musical talents to self-support by singing in the streets and doorsteps. That is how he met a benefactress, Frau Ursula Cotta. She treated Martin as her adopted son. This gesture of an unknown woman's affectionate tutelage played an important role in lifting Martin further up to aspire for university education in Erfurt at the age of 18. Guidance and support from good hearted families and people were instrumental in Martin's development as a father of Protestant Reformation in God-appointed time.

Pastor Aaron

Aaron was the first Indian protestant pastor ordained on 28th December 1733. He was born in an orthodox Hindu family in the coastal town of Cuddalore in Tamil Nadu. His parents named him Arumugam after one of the famous Hindu deities. During his childhood, catechist Savarimuthu guided Arumugam in schooling and learning the scriptures. When the family struggled in poverty due to loss in business, Arumugam went to Tranquebar, 70 km from Cuddalore, where he met Bartholomaus Ziegenbalg, the first Protestant Missionary in India, and grew up under his tutelage. On 5th August, 1718, Arumugam was baptized by Ziegenbalg and given the name Aaron.

K.S. Amos in the biography of Pastor Aaron writes, "Ziegenbalg helped him understand the biblical concept of discipleship or following the Lord...and appointed him as a school master in the Tamil school to teach writing and counting." The tutelage provided by the catechist Savarimuthu and Ziegenbalg facilitated holistic development in the life of child Arumugam amidst family crisis.

Vedanayagam Sastriyar

Vedanayagam Sastriyar is one of the legends in Tamil Christian Literature and music ministry. His lyrics are sung in mainline churches of CSI and TELC even today. Vedanayagam was born on 7th September 1774 in Thirunelveli, Tamil Nadu. His father Arunachalam Pillai was a landlord. He was the head of local administration of a Siva Temple in the village. When Vedanayagam was seven years old, his mother passed away. However, his father did his best to develop his son through tuitions. In 1783, his father employed a tutor to instruct him in Literature and Mathematics. At one point of time, Vedanayagam detested the tuition. On seeing his father praying for him tearfully, Vedanayagam changed his mind and became determined to study and develop.

There was a German missionary and statesman Rev. C.F. Schwartz (1726-1798) in Thanjavur who was known for his humanitarian services particularly for children in vulnerable environment. It so happened that C.F. Schwartz visited Vedanayagam's place and met him.

"My dear child, what's your name?" Schwartz asked in Tamil with a bright smile on his face. He was well versed in more than one language.

"Vedanayagam," replied the young boy of twelve. He was quite surprised to see a white man speaking his mother tongue.

Schwartz found something special as he read the face of the boy. He could see that God has bestowed talents abundantly on the village child Vedanayagam.

"Vedanayagam, are you interested to study more?"

"Yes.," he replied with confidence.

"Then you must come with me to Tanjore. You can stay in the children's home and go to school," Schwartz said with big dreams about the boy. Somehow, he knew one day Vedanayagam would be a man of Christian witnessing in this land. There was no response from the boy, but he looked at his father for the answer. The missionary repeated the same question again and this time looking at the boy's father.

"Will you send your son with me now? I will do everything to educate him and God will bless your son."

After few seconds Arunachalam Pillai gave his consent.

The missionary brought Vedanayagam to Tanjore where he excelled in education, particularly in Tamil Literature. All through his life he composed a variety of gospel poems and songs in classical Tamil.

The tutelage of his father, a local tutor and the missionary, were significant contributions to Vedanayagam's becoming a renowned Christian poet and evangelist.

William Carey

It was a Sunday afternoon. Edmund Carey was looking for his son William Carey to pass on a message.

"William..William..where are you?"

"He is outside under the tree" his mother gave direction.

"What on the earth is the little boy doing there?" exclaimed Edmund. He opened the backyard door and found William sitting in the shade of the tree and reading a book.

"Hey William! Come on.. I got a message for you."

At once William ran to his father with the book. His father asked him for the book to have a look at it.

"This is all about the sea voyages of Columbus. Are you going to do it yourself?"

William did not answer his father's question but asked him, "What is the message for me?"

By this time his mother had joined them. His father took William's hands and said, "My son, you must undertake an apprenticeship in shoe making from next week. So get ready. Shoe making is a promising trade nowadays."

The fourteen-year-old lad joined the apprenticeship at Potters Pury, 8 miles from his village Paulerspury. That was a turning point in his life.

Edmund Carey was a poor weaver in the village Paulerspury in Northampton, England. He also taught in the village school after the death of his father Peter Carey, who was the first teacher of the village school. Edmund's mother was in deep grief as the death of her eldest son William caused the death of her husband the very next month. The wedding of Edmund with Elizabeth brought in comfort to Edmund's mother as her daughter in law plainly displayed the characters of Ruth in the Bible. The family lived happily in a thatched house and they were blessed with a boy child, William Carey, on 10th November 1761. Edmund, as a lover of books and children, was highly skilful in teaching arithmetic and Christian truths from the Bible. It is not wrong to conclude that Carey inherited all such skills from his father. Even as a schoolboy Carey was conscious of serving others. He often fetched water for the family from a spring across the road, and firewood from the Whittlebury forest at the village border.

Edmund had an elder brother, Peter Carey, who was away in Canada for many years. One fine morning, Peter showed up at Edmund's doorstep. Child Carey found a wonderful tutor in Peter soon. Peter would narrate stories about Canada and sea voyages and natural beauties which little Carey cherished much. Carey, most likely, developed a mind of curiosity about plants and flowers from his uncle Peter.

Carey had given himself to reading of books about sea voyages. Christopher Columbus was his hero and he was nicknamed after the same name by his friends. Carey was given every opportunity by his family to read, learn, experiment, adventure, and even take part in the village church choir. At the age of 12, Carey fell ill which forced on him a time of quarantine for almost two years. During this time, Carey learnt to be determined and focused.

During Carey's shoe making apprenticeship in Potterspury, he came in contact with one John Warr who was three years older. Warr led Carey to the saving knowledge of Jesus Christ by taking him to prayer meetings. Another person who played a remarkable role in the development of Carey was Tom Jones. Jones tutored Carey in learning Greek and provided him with a Greek glossary-grammar. Having been under caring tutelage of his parents, uncle, teachers, trainers and friends, there is no wonder that William Carey came to be known as the Father of Modern Missions after his forty years of mission work in Bengal.

Louis Braille

Louis Braille is known for his invention of code letters to enable the blind to read and write. Louis Braille was born on January 4, 1809, in a small village of Coupvray, 25 kilometres from Paris. His parents were poor. Braille lost his eyesight when he was three years old. It was the tutorial efforts of his father Simon that caused Loius to develop an interest in learning. Abbe Polluy, the Catholic priest of the village Coupvray, tutored Braille in basic education. There was many a risky situation in the life of child Louis. Visually challenged children were ill-treated those days and they were sent out for begging. Child Louis escaped from bomb attacks during the war between France and Austria in 1814.

Fanny Crosby

Fanny Crosby was born on March 24th, 1820, in Putnam County near New York. Fanny Crosby's mother Mercy Crosby supported her family by working as a house maid since her father John Crosby died before Fanny was one year old.

When Fanny was born, her parents John Crosby and Mercy were incredibly grateful to God for their child Fanny. They never expected the tragedy that would befall the life of the six weeks old infant. Little Fanny was crying nonstop one rainy day. She was not well for the past few days. The local physician had prescribed medicine for chest cold and it did not seem to be effective.

"John, please check with the doctor immediately. There is something wrong with her eyes. She is not able to open her eyes." Mercy pleaded.

John returned soon.

"Mercy, our doctor is out of station in New York, but there is a new one nearby. Let's go see him."

After a downpour that morning, it was still drizzling.

The doctor pointed out at once, "She is suffering from eye infection."

"But Doctor, she has been having a running nose for a few days and this is what our doctor prescribed before," John showed the paper. But the physician did not take much notice of it.

Seriously examining the eyes of Fanny, he said, "It's alright. But now, her eyes need attention"

The physician put a drop of solution in each eye which brought the child's crying to an end. John and Mercy looked at each other and nodded.

"Bring her again tomorrow. I will check and if necessary, put the eye drops again," the physician said confidently.

Mercy was quite upset to see that her daughter's eyes remained closed the whole day. She could tell that the child was not able to keep her eyes open even for a moment.

The next day they visited the physician again and he put the eye drops again. The running nose stopped but she could not open her eyes and look around. "What did the young physician do to our child?", they thought. On the third day they heard that the young physician had left the village for good. Their family physician returned and confirmed that her eye sight was lost. It was a shock for the parents, but they had faith on the God they believed in. Yes, God had a different purpose for that child, Fanny Crosby, for she grew up to be the person who has penned more gospel songs than anyone in history.

In her autobiography, Fanny mentions three people who took personal interest in her development and tutored her. The first one was her grandmother; the second was Mrs. Hawley with whom Fanny and her mother stayed; and the third was Mr. Hamilton Murray, a Board member of the New York Institution for the Blind.

About her grandmother Fanny writes, "My grandmother was a woman of exemplary piety and from her I learnt many useful and abiding lessons. She was a firm believer in prayer; and when I was very young, taught me to believe that our Father in heaven will always give us whatever is for our good."

Narrating her learning experience from Mrs. Hawley, Fanny writes, "Mrs. Hawley became deeply interested in me, and under her supervision I acquired a thorough knowledge of the Bible." Recollecting Mr. Hamilton's tutoring her on poems Fanny writes, "He read to me from the classics by the hour and advised me to commit long passages to memory; and frequently he gave me the lines of favourite poets to imitate." Tutorial efforts of her grandmother, the house owner and the Board member contributed to the HCD of child Fanny Crosby.

Pandit Ramabai

Childhood of Pandit Ramabai was full of hardships. But there were people who provided the needed tutelage for her holistic development. Ramabai was born on 23th April, 1858, as the youngest child of Anant Shastri Dongre and his second wife Lakshmibai in a forest home. They were Brahmins whose ancestors had prominent positions in the courts of the kings of Maharashtra. Ramabai's father Anant Shastri was well versed in Sanskrit and he was an itinerant, reciting *Puranas* in temples, which fetched him income for livelihood. He was the first tutor in the life of Ramabai. She was taught Sanskrit and the Hindu scriptures by her father for the act of which her father was condemned by the Brahmin Council. During the famine of 1876-77, she lost her parents and sisters. She was left with her elder brother Srinivas.

Under the care of her brother, Ramabai came to Calcutta in 1878 where she was conferred with the titles of Pandit and Saraswati by Sanskrit scholars. Keshab Chandra Sen, a social reformer, provided her with the religious books of Hindu tradition.

She could master those literatures in no time and found there was something missing in them as to her quest for life purpose and meaning. Her brother Srinivas died in 1880. She married a lawyer and soon became a widow with a girl child at the age of 23. The Christian organization 'Mukthi Mission' at Kedgoan, near Pune in Maharashtra, was founded by Pandit Ramabai in 1889. Till date the organization continues to care for widows, girl children, visually challenged and abandoned women.

When Ramabai was in Assam living with her husband, a Baptist evangelist Isaac Allen visited her regularly and gave her a copy of the Gospel of Luke. But it was in 1883 in England when Ramabai was converted to Christianity on her own accord. When she returned to India she was known as a Christian Missionary committed to availing every means of educating women and children in Indian context. In spite of all the ill fortunes all through her childhood, there were people who stood by her and gave her support to survive and develop to be a reformer in her later lifetime.

Amy Carmichael

Amy Beatrice Carmichael was born on 16th December, 1867, in a sea-coast village of Mill Isle in Northern Ireland. Her parents were David Carmichael and Catherine Jane Filson. Amy was the eldest of seven children. Her parents were keen on tutoring children on the Bible and Shorter Catechism. When Amy was a small girl she used to pray that God would come and sit by her side on the sheet spread on the floor beside her. Amy was not happy about her brown eyes since blue eyes were natural for them.

"Mummy, I don't want my brown eyes. I want blue eyes like my friends," a strong complaint came from child Amy.

"No dear, it is God given, you understand that," her mother replied with a loving smile.

"All my friends make fun of me. I am praying about this for many days. But God is not answering," tears pooled in the brown eyes of Amy. Her mother gave her a hug, patted her back and let her go after kissing her daughter.

Even at the age of three, Amy was taught by her mother that answers from God might be a 'No' or a 'Silence.' Amy found the answer for her brown eyes when she came to Tamil Nadu as a missionary. Because of her brown eyes, which were similar to Tamil women, she was able to move through the villages rescuing children of temple prostitutes.

Apart from her parents, Amy had an opportunity of being tutored by a sincere teacher Eleanor Milne. Eleanor, a hired tutor, would come to Amy's house for teaching the children. Amy enjoyed

Eleanor's reciting poems, discussions about caring for animals, narrating stories of martyrs and the church history of England and Scotland.

At a point of time, Amy's father got struck with financial crisis due to troubles in running his mills. So, the family moved to another town. Amy had to go to Wesleyan Methodist Boarding School in Harrogate, Yorkshire. For a lover of nature like Amy, the strict rules and regulations of the boarding school were mere obstacles to freedom of enjoying the beauty of God's creation. It was here in 1883 that Amy gave her life to Jesus Christ after the preaching of the evangelist Edwin Arrowsmith. In 1885, when Amy was 18, her father died of continuous illness. Then onwards she began to look forward to serving her Lord as a missionary. Finally, she landed in Tamil Nadu in 1895 and founded the Donahvur Fellowship that continues to serve girl children from vulnerable life situations today.

Ida Scudder

Ida's parents, Dr. John Scudder and Sophia were serving the Lord as medical missionaries in the Arcot district of Tamil Nadu when Ida was born on 6th December 1870. Her parents were busy introducing a weaving and spinning school in Ranipet at this time. When Ida was 8 years old, a devastating famine in 1878 took the lives of people and cattle in thousands. Dr. Scudder and Sophia had given themselves fully to relief distributions. With deaths all around, Ida learnt from her parents to face every situation in life without fear.

Dr. John Scudder's failing health led the family back to America for rejuvenation. In 1882, when Ida was 12 years, her father returned to India to continue the medical mission. Life was pleasant and sweet for Ida because of the presence of her mother. Two years had gone by since her father went to India leaving his wife and children behind in America when one day during a play time in the evening, Ida's mother called her children to the drawing room.

"Children, don't be alarmed by what I am going to say to you now."

All the children got closer to her looking at her mouth expecting what she was going to say.

"I must go to India to help your father in the mission. And we have made all arrangements for you to continue your education here. Keep praying. God will be with you. I will be really missing you dear." She left for India within a few days.

In the absence of her parents, Ida found warmth and love in the family of Uncle Henry in Chigaco. Soon she was admitted into the Seminary for Girls run by the great evangelist Dwight L. Moody in Massachusetts. Ida later wrote about her reminiscences and how she was strengthened by the prayers of D.L. Moody. This was the place where she grew up to be a woman of loving nature and humanity with sportive spirits.

In another two years, Ida was summoned to India to help her ill-stricken mother. She landed back in India after eight years, when she was sixteen. That was the time God gave her the vision of founding a medical school for women and a hospital in Vellore which developed to be the famous Christian Medical College (CMC) in Vellore today. From the history of her ancestors, we know that they were medical missionaries. There is no doubt that this was one of the motivating influences on her to become a medical missionary herself.

A GAIN

*Contemporary Tuition Centres
in Chennai Slums and HCD*

CHAPTER 9

Tuition Centre 1: Obligation of Great Commission

In this section, attention is drawn to the existing tuition centres in Chennai slums. We will discuss in the forthcoming four chapters how these contemporary tuition centres are able to contribute to HCD and what issues and challenges they encounter. Two centres run by mission organizations and another two centres run by local churches have been selected for the study. We will then draw some conclusions from what we learnt from the study, in the final chapter.

Tuition centre 1

The children of this centre came from the slums of Lock Street, Davidpuram, Pumping Station, Sannyasipuram, Medawakam, Swamidaspuram, Kellys, Kannagi Nagar and Ayanavaram. Most of the children were from the Lock Street slum. It was a wonderful sight to see the children coming to these centres with hope. Most of the children here went to government schools or government aided private management schools. This tuition centre was one of such centres all over India run by an international mission.

Interviewee of the Tuition centre 1 was the Manager of the centre. He was very cooperative and patient in answering my questions. Our meetings took place in the centre which was inside a Church compound. It was the principle of the Mission to have the tuition centres in churches only since it believed that the Church is the God appointed agency through which a child can develop holistically. The interview schedule is given in Appendix 1.

Slum, Children and Families

At the time of the research, there were about 1500 families in Lock Street slum. Most of them worked as labourers, auto drivers and petty shop keepers. Some of them worked as casual labourers in Mental Health Hospital and Tamil Nadu Water and Sewage Board. The women worked as house maids in the neighbourhood. Jothi and Sujatha, two mothers in Lock Street slum pointed out that children were highly vulnerable to immorality from a young age. For them, the tuition centre was a safe haven for the children. A few private tuition centres were run in houses on payment basis in the slum. Children attended the Corporation School and Tamil Baptist Church Elementary school in Kilpauk, Bentinck School and St. Paul's school in Vepery and Bala Naidu Girls School and Muthaia Chettiar School in Purasaiwakam. People generally had access to several private clinics in the vicinity. A Public Health Centre in Kilpauk Gardens provided health services. For major treatments, people went to Kilpauk Medical College Hospital. There was a mini park available on the roadside.

Churches, Government and NGO

About 10 independent Pentecostal churches and two Roman Catholic churches were present in the slum. Tamil Baptist Church, IELC Good Shepherd Church, TELC Arulnathar Church, Sr. Saral Navaroji Fellowship and the Pentecostal Mission Church are located in the neighbourhood of the slum. Street taps were provided for drinking water. A public toilet was available. Almost every household had a toilet attached to their house. There was a functioning Government Balwadi in the area. No NGO services were at work in Lock Street at the time of the research.

Organization

The mission statement of the organization was: 'Releasing children from poverty in Jesus' name: In response to the Great Commission, this mission organization exists as an advocate for children, to release them from their spiritual, economic, social and physical poverty and enable them to become responsible and fulfilled Christian adults'. According to the pastor of the Church where the tuition centre was located, it was a gateway to evangelize slum children and the community by expressing the love of God through various efforts of helping children to come up in life.

Tuition Centre

The tuition centre has been organized in a local church since 2002. It was officially known as Child Development Centre (CDC). The centre was open from 4:30pm to 7pm from Monday to Friday. On Saturdays, special programs were organized for children and parents. There were 271 children on roll. Children studying in 2nd class and above were admitted into the tuition. Children were given care and support up to the age of 22 years. Eight tutors and two administrative staff were engaged in facilitating the development of children. Tutors were designated as Child Development Facilitators.

A system was in place for day to day administration of tuition centre, headed by the Manager. An advisory committee with the Pastor as the Chairman monitored the centre as per the instructions provided by the mission organization. The mission organization conducted periodical reviews of child development process and audit of accounts. Funding for the tuition centre was provided by the international mission organization. According to the interviewee, the purpose of the tuition centres was to facilitate Holistic Child Development.

Child Friendly Environment

There was adequate space available for study, indoor games, outdoor games and creative activities like drawing and music. Facilities like book room, toilets, clean drinking water and First Aid box were available. Staff were periodically trained on child care and maintaining a friendly relationship with children and parents. The staff–children ratio was maintained at 1:30. This was fairly ideal for facilitating and monitoring HCD of each child. The staff members of tuition centre were periodically trained for capacity building in understanding children and their rights so that they kept the environment child friendly.

Case Stories

Success Story

Prabakaran [name changed], born in a Hindu family of Samidaspuram slum, was brought to the tuition centre by his mother since his father, an auto rickshaw driver, abandoned the family when he was eight years old. His mother earned her livelihood by working as a maid in the neighbourhood. Prabakaran was a slow learner and a malnourished child. Frequent counselling was needed to lead him out of psychological problems due to his family situations. Being loved by the people in the tuition centre led Prabakaran to know Jesus personally. He grew to be a successful football player in State level and soon became an active youth member in the church. Now he is employed in an IT company. Through him the family has come to faith in Jesus.

Failure Story

Jasmine's parents died when she was a child and her grandmother took care of her. Jasmine from Lock Street slum came to the tuition centre when she was in 2nd standard. She was given all care and support by the tuition centre to the extent of getting her admission in Bentinck school, one of the best schools in Chennai. When she was in 9th standard she fell in love with a boy. Counselling by the tuition staff to overcome adolescence challenges helped her to enter 10th standard. Yet she could not resist the emotional pressure and she eloped with that boy making her life miserable. It is learnt that she was abandoned by the boy. In spite of several attempts by tuition staff, Jasmine's development was interrupted by situations that led her astray. She was physically and mentally healthy but her spiritual and psycho-social developments were not adequately formed.

Educating Parents on HCD

Children from Hindu families number 100 and constituted a large percentage of the total number of children on roll. About 40 children came from Christian families. Once a month meetings with parents were convened to discuss topics of child rearing with reference to health, prevention of diseases, healthy food habits, education, child psychology, adolescence issues and income generation. Family Retreats were organized every year to help parents grow in spiritual life. Career guidance was provided. There is a Love and Care Fellowship program organized for families of other faiths where love of God in Jesus Christ was practically communicated.

Holistic Child Development

Spiritual Development

Challenges

It was found that 80% of children in the tuition do not show interest in spiritual development. This was primarily due to parents' negligence in this area of child growth. Peer pressure was discovered to be another force that challenged spiritual growth of slum children.

Monitoring

Participation of children in spiritual activities like recitation of memory verses, prayer, Bible contests and change of behaviour were observed by staff and recorded in the register.

Core Activities

Daily prayer time schedule was followed. Periodic rallies, retreats and camps were organized. Children took part in VBS and Christmas programs. House prayers in the communities were arranged once a week. Christian missions of Youth For Christ (YFC), Evangelical Union (EU) and Scripture Union (SU) were invited to minister to the children in the tuition centre. Children were encouraged to go to nearby local churches.

Physical Development

Challenges

Lack of nutritious food and ignorance of parents about providing proper diet to children were the basic causes for the physical problems that children underwent. Since most of the mothers were house maids, they brought home leftover food from the houses they worked in. To save time, parents expected children to buy food from roadside vendors that are kept in unhygienic environment. Following their parents' model, children did not prefer healthy food and hygienic practices such as washing of hands before meals and trimming the nails regularly as needed. About 80% of the children did not have breakfast. Only during festivals did children get good meals.

Monitoring

Body Mass Index of children was calculated every three months by registering height and weight ratio with reference to the standard chart based on age. This practice is helpful to identify health problems like malnourishment or overweight. Once in four months, health screening was done and the results recorded. The service of doctors from outside the organisation was availed for Annual Health Check-up of the children and necessary steps were taken for treatment. Separate formats were employed to record the parameters.

Core Activities

It was the aim of the mission that every child should be physically healthy. Every day children were served snacks prepared with pulses before tuition and nutritious meal prepared with cereals after tuition classes in the evening. Children coming for morning classes were served milk before they went to school. Every week special addresses were made on personal hygiene like washing of hands, dental care, wearing clean clothes, food habits and inner wear cleanliness. Physical exercise was given importance for both boys and girls. Space in the church compound was used for outdoor games like Kho-kho, Volleyball and Badminton. Children benefitted from medical camps organized by local churches. A group of doctors from other faiths were invited to give awareness to children on physical development. The mission was in contact with the Apollo Hospitals and Sundaram Medical Foundation for treatment of major illness with concession in fees. Awareness programs for children on TB, Malaria and HIV/AIDS were organized by the TB Hospital in Chennai. Boys interested in gymnastics and games like football were sent to coaching classes.

Cognitive Development

Challenges

Illiterate parents, wrong role models in family and community, parents with no focus and vision for children development, low capacity of children for schooling and lack of opportunities for developing knowledge and talents were discovered to be the causes for the problems that challenge cognitive development.

Monitoring

The mission used a Multiple-Intelligence Tool where the level of interest a child had for education and talent development were measured. Marks scored by the child in Unit Tests and Cycle Tests were recorded. Progress Card from schools was recorded to assess the performance of the child in school.

Core Activities

Individual attention was given for completing homework. Periodic Unit Test and Cycle Test were conducted. Slow learners were identified and given extra care and coaching. The mission took care of fees in schools and colleges. Special coaching classes were conducted for the children appearing for 10th and 12th standard exams. For children interested in music, Vocal and Keyboard classes were arranged. A library for children was available in the centre.

Bible based contests in singing, elocution; debate, drawing and quiz were organized to develop talents in children. Children were taken on educational tour to museums, Science parks and planetariums.

During Open Day meetings in schools, tutors met the school authorities on behalf of parents to know about the child's performance and behaviour. Before completing 12th standard, the child in mid-adolescence received at least two employable skills like tailoring, computer operation, hardware mechanism and mobile phones repairing.

For training children in employable skills, outside agencies were used for which the mission meets the expenses. Funds from Corporate Social Response (CSR) department of companies were raised to support higher education. Children were given awareness on ecological balance and harmfulness of plastics by an NGO called EXNORA.

Social Development

Challenges

There were no role models in family as well as in the community of slums for children to admire and follow. Peer groups were another effective cause that challenged social development of slum children. Politicians treat slum communities as vote bank and give money to keep a group of youth around them. This has led to many youths falling into social evils of unproductive living, addiction, immorality, gang life and theft.

Monitoring
The mission employed a tool by the name Quality Life to record verbal and behavioural quality of children. This format was upgraded periodically in order to monitor the social development of a child.

Core Activities
The mission followed a curriculum available for facilitating children's social development. Lessons were provided to suit age-wise needs and challenges. Children were encouraged and trained to take part in school events like School day, Sports day and talent contests. Engaging in indoor games like Puzzles, Carom board, Chess and Building blocks was helpful for social development of children in understanding self control, friendship, success and failure.

Children's participation

College students in the tuition centre helped school students in their studies. Child Parliament activities were encouraged. Children were consulted while planning Christmas programmes, camps and retreats. Leadership qualities were developed by assigning responsibilities to organize events in the tuition centre.

Caring for Adolescents

Age-wise curriculum was used for imparting **Life Coping Skills** in adolescent children. Boys and girls were counselled in groups as well as individually. Children manifesting irresponsible behaviour were referred to counselling specialists. Such initiatives brought out changed behaviour in society and improved performance in schools. Tutors used special guide book once a week to teach children on understanding adolescence. Once in three months, adolescents were given counselling by doctors and counsellors. Audio-Visual materials were used twice a year to educate them on adolescence.

Patriotism and Secular resources

Children were encouraged to take part in national days events conducted in their respective schools. Secular resource materials like newspapers and Tamil Weeklies were provided for the reading of children. Due to budget restrictions, secular resources of children books or Audio Visual materials were no longer used in the tuition centre.

Networking

Staff of other Christian NGOs were invited to teach Life Coping Skills once a week. Volunteers were invited to visit the centre to give career guidance as and when need arises.

Critical Analysis

Unit 1: Purpose, implementation and resource

According to the interviewees, the overall purpose of the tuition centre was to facilitate HCD of slum children. This purpose was fulfilled to its minute details. Also, this mission had a particularly good experience of more than thirteen years in running tuition centre. The mission statement mentioned that mission was an advocate for children at risk. But, thus far, the mission had no contact with local churches around Chennai slums to motivate and guide them to run tuition centres.

Admission of children into the centre was restricted. It was dependent on the fund allotted to each child. In this case, there is a possibility that many more needy children in slums are left out. More children could be benefitted by need-based interventions than fund driven interventions. Implementation of tuition was carried out by the mission with partnership of the local church that had adequate space for children. Also, this partnership supplemented to the mission task of the local church. However, instead of having the centre in the church compound, organizing tuition centre in the slums could avert the common accusation on the Church with regards to conversion.

Financial support for the centre was provided by a foreign agency. This implied that the centre will run as long as it was supported from an external source. This must be viewed seriously and ways to sustain the centre with local resources in future must be considered. This raised the question of sustainability. One solution would be to encourage parents to contribute towards meeting some expenses. However, this need not be mandatory since there may be some in deep economic straits.

Unit 2: Challenges to HCD and families

As per the interviewee, most of the challenges to HCD a child in slum faces were from a child's own family. The mission took the initiative for educating parents on HCD. Again, all these activities were convened inside the church compound and restricted to parents of the children on roll in the centre. What about other parents? Why were parents' meetings not arranged in a common place like community room in the slum? 'Church compound centeredness' needs to be avoided otherwise it may be viewed suspiciously by the people and government. Entering church compounds has been currently, at the time of this writing, prohibited or severe restrictions have been enforced as we are in the days of national lock down for the global pandemic Covid-19. Could this be God teaching us a lesson?

Most of the resource persons addressing the parents were people with a church background like pastors and evangelists. Attempting to organize parents' meetings in slums with resource persons of other faiths from the fields of health, employment and government schemes would be more relevant. Otherwise, there was a risk for tuition centres being misunderstood for nurturing religious fundamentalism.

Unit 3: Role of tuition centre in facilitating HCD

Various tools of formats were in place to measure the HCD of each child. Information was recorded in respective registers and follow up is carried on. All the aspects of HCD viz. spiritual, physical, cognitive and social were attended to by the centre. One of the positive aspects seen in this tuition centre was that children's participation in organizing events was encouraged. Networking was adopted within Christian circles to carry on activities with respect to all elements of HCD. The centre could make use of secular books and periodicals for cognitive and social development of children. Adequate emphasis was not given to celebrate national days. During national days, special events like essay writing, singing, elocution and poems writing on themes of nation building could be organized.

Unit 4: Opportunities and Challenges to mission

Most of the children came from families of other faiths. It was discovered that through the tuition centre, more children from outside the church were able to know Christ. It remained a favourable platform for mission but parents in slums were not particular about the spiritual development of their children. This was the major challenge to the mission. All their attention was to escape from poverty. While economic welfare is desirable, on the other hand, Christian perspective on poverty needs to be passed on to them. We can also recognize that it is not easy today in a context where Christian TV preachers promoting prosperity teachings is largely prevalent.

CHAPTER 10

Tuition Centre 2: Transforming India for Christ

The second mission organization in the study is an indigenous national level mission organization, running tuition centres in many states of India. It is a charitable Christian mission organization serving India since 1999. It worked through local churches for the transformation of people in need. The tuition centre in an independent church hall in Pallavan Nagar slum was one of the 40 tuition centres run by this mission in Chennai. The officials in the central administrative office elsewhere were kind enough to permit me to visit this centre to meet children and parents. The pastor of the church in the slum could not make it to the centre during my visits for ministry reasons. Finally he consented to an appointment in a place about 5 kms away from Pallavan Nagar slum. All through the interview process, the Area Coordinator, a young man working in the mission as promotional staff, set apart his time to meet me. Even he could not come to the place of tuition centres and asked me to meet him elsewhere, away from the slum.

Slum, Children and Families

Pallavan Nagar slum, located near Chindadiripet Railway Station, was spread along the Northern bank of Cooum River, a few kilometres before it merges with the Bay of Bengal. There were about 800 families here. Men earned their livelihood by driving autorickshaws, goods carrier tri-wheelers and other works in construction sites. In many families, fathers proved to be the most irresponsible models for the children. Though children showed interest in college education, their parents were unable to pay the fees.

Children were found to be willing to study and develop. However, children, particularly girls, run short of time for school homework since they are expected to do household chores both in the morning and the evening. Awareness about access to government schemes for education was lacking among the habitants.

The children attended CSI Monagan Higher Secondary School in Rayapetta, CSI Wesley School in Triplicane, Corporation School in Chetpat, Kalyana Higher Secondary School in Chindadripet, and St. Augustine Middle School in Chindadiripet. All these schools are funded by the Government. Rajiv Gandhi General Hospital and few private clinics were accessed by the people. There was no playground or any recreation activities for the children.

Church, Government and NGO

There were a few independent churches in the area. A few Christian families attended Assembly of God Church (AG) in Saidapet and Apostolic Christian Assembly (ACA) in Purasaivakkam.

The Government runs a Balwadi centre. A functioning public toilet unit was in a corner of the slum. With dissatisfaction and disappointment parents stated that it was not adequate for the population. Corporation water supply was provided every alternative day. World Vision worked here for seven years. Samithi for Education Environment and Social Health Action (SEESHA), a sister concern of Jesus Calls ministry in Chennai, conducted monthly prayer meetings for four years. At the time of the research, there was no NGO operating in the area.

Organization

The vision of the mission was stated as 'Making Disciples to transform India for Christ.' The mission ran about 40 tuition centres in and around Chennai through local churches. The mission statement read: 'To assist Indian Churches and Missions in their endeavours to establish transformed communities in a systematic and measurable way. This was accomplished through spiritual, physical, social and economic transformation through the programs.' According to the interviewee, the purpose of the tuition centre was to introduce Jesus Christ to the children both inside and outside the church.

Tuition Centre

The mission ran a tuition centre in an independent church hall. The tuition centre was named 'After School Club' under Children and Youth Development Program (CYDP) of the mission. The centre has been functioning for the past four years. The centre was located inside the slum. It was open from 5pm to 7pm from Monday to Friday. Forty children from class 1 to class 9 were benefitted by the centre. Most of them went to government schools.

One tutor was appointed who was responsible for helping children in studies. The tutor was designated as Club Leader. The mission appoints the Club Leader and monitors the functioning of the centre through periodic visits by an Area Coordinator. The day to day activity was monitored by the pastor of the local church. Training programs for pastors and tutors were organized annually.

Child Friendly Environment

Play items were made available. The centre utilized the hall of the Prayer House that was spacious and airy. It was maintained clean and litter free. Tutors were trained once a year where they were taught child rights, child psychology and child development.

Case Stories

Success Story

David's father died of alcoholism. His mother worked as house maid. His father comes from a Roman Catholic background and mother from a Hindu family. David came to the tuition centre and showed good improvement in his studies and conduct. David immediately began to attend church services and Sunday Classes regularly. His elder brother had to stop his education after 10th Class in order to meet family needs out of daily wages jobs. David could complete a post graduation with the help of his brother's support. He currently works in an electronic company. David was involved in the tuition centre by helping school children get through exams.

Failure Story

Child Kalaivani came to tuition centre when she was in Class 6. Her father is an alcoholic and mother works as sanitary labour in the Corporation. Kalaivani did well in studies and attended Sunday Classes till she reached 10th class. She stopped attending tuition and Sunday Classes regularly thereafter. She was found to be going around with boyfriends. In spite of frequent counselling by the tutor and the Pastor, there was no change in her behaviour. She could not get through 11th Class and now she stays at home.

Educating Parents on HCD

About 30 children were from Hindu families and 10 from Christian families. This mission had the policy of focussing on children only. No events were conducted for parents.

Holistic Child Development

Spiritual Development

Challenges

Parents were often discovered to be the major cause for the spiritual problems of the children. They prevented their children from going to churches because of their superstitious belief that change of faith would bring curses from their deities. Poverty makes them question God and leading to disbelief. Religious festivals and celebrations attracted children.

Monitoring

Involvement of each child in spiritual activities was observed keenly but no records were maintained for this purpose. Some children who were initially known to neglect spiritual activities in the past later exhibit seriousness towards spiritual development. Church going children were identified for spiritual nurture through counselling and prayer.

Core Activities

After study time, there was a time for prayer at 6:30 pm. Recitation of memory verses by children took place on weekly basis. Bible Story Books were presented to children every year. Children Bible Club was organized once a year during summer holidays. The local church pastor was kept informed about children who were interested to know Jesus Christ.

Networking

No outside agency was utilized for the spiritual development of children except the local church where the tuition centre was run.

Physical Development

Challenges

Lack of nutritious food due to parents' negligence was the major cause for health problems of children. For many families, healthy food was beyond their affordability because of poor income. Congested housing, irregular supply of drinking water, contamination of water, improper drainage system and open defecation were the causes of health crisis among children. At times children skipped bathing altogether for want of water.

Monitoring

No monitoring activity was carried out. Overall health condition of children was observed in general. Children who did not take baths were listed out for individual counselling.

Core Activities

Every Friday mass counselling on health and hygiene like bathing regularly, hand washing, nail cutting and keeping the environment clean was given. No special intervention was undertaken regarding adolescent children who were susceptible to deviant behaviour with respect to spurts in their physical growth, understanding the opposite sex, overcoming peer pressure for substance abuse, and personal hygiene.

Networking

As stated earlier, no networking was attempted as per the policy. Though the mission did not bring in any service provider from outside for physical development of the children, voluntary involvement by other churches was welcome. Distribution of snacks, medical camps and awareness programs on health could be organized by churches.

Cognitive Development

Challenges

Children did not have favourable environment in houses due to the absence of quietness and space. Family quarrels and street clashes disturbed their attention on studies. Some school going children resorted to part time rag-picking work. Peer pressure and poverty prevented them from pursuing college education. In government schools, children did not get individual attention and assistance to get through exams. There were instances of children experiencing caste discriminations in these schools.

Monitoring

Information given by the children on the marks scored in tests and exams were taken note of by the tutor. Assistance was given to children who needed to improve. Children were expected to come up with self motivation in seeking tutor's help for getting more marks in school.

Core Activities

Assisting children to complete homework was given top priority in the centre. Many children were not able to meet this need since they lacked basic knowledge of primary subjects of Tamil, English and Mathematics. Not having adequate stationery like pens and note books to do home work was another issue. Children were encouraged to pray to Jesus for wisdom. Extra time was spent by the tutor to help children score good marks. Tests were conducted every two months.

Networking

As a matter of policy, the mission did not network with outside agencies. Any attempt by the local pastor to engage a tutor from outside required monetary expenditure by way of fees to the tutor and travel charges.

Social Development

Challenges

The deviant social lifestyle of adults, peer pressure and lack of contact with outer world were the hindrances to social development of children. It is quite common that marriages of sons/daughters are arranged by families of one slum with the sons/daughters of families of another slum. Children born to such couple naturally have no other way than to grow under the influences of psycho-socio environments in slums. The slum family cycle continues.

Monitoring

Attending church services regularly was considered an indication of social development on the whole. Often children reported family fighting. It was observed that by the time children reach 7th and 8thgradesin school, they began to display adult habits of smoking, drinking, bullying young children and perpetuating gangster trend. Whistle blowers among the children informed the tutor about any misbehaviour in school.

Core Activities

An informal individual and mass counselling session was organised every two months on taking care of personality development by proper dressing, neat appearance and cultured behaviour in words and actions. Importance of morality in community life of family, friends circle, school and neighbourhood was emphasised. Immediate attention was given to children living in problematic family situations like homes with single parent, separated parents or homes with domestic violence. Opportunities to play sports like Football, Volleyball, Cricket and Badminton were given for boys; girls were provided with Ring ball and Skipping ropes. Engaging in such sports activities enhanced social growth of the children.

Children's participation

Children were involved in programs during Easter and Christmas. Their opinions and ideas were included while planning programs. Group leaders were given the responsibility of keeping play items in the tuition centre. Children who passed out from tuition centre earlier were actively involved in helping the present children in studies.

Caring for Adolescents

There were no regular activities in this regard. There was no one available in the local church to handle this issue. The local pastor handled certain issues related to boys as and when required. In the case of girls, the need remained unmet.

Patriotism and Secular Resources

During his visit, the Area Coordinator informally enquired the children about attending national flag hoisting events in schools. Regarding utilizing secular resources like periodicals for children in Tamil and English, the Coordinator responded in the negative.

Networking

Outside agencies were not engaged in facilitating social development of children in the tuition centre. As far as the local pastor was concerned, anyone from churches outside the slum could come forward and avail the opportunity to minister to the children regarding their psycho-socio development.

Critical Analysis

Unit 1: Purpose, implementation and resources

According to the purpose statement given by the interviewee, evangelism was the dominant objective of running the tuition centre. It would be relevant if the management of the mission realigned its goals to the need of slum children that are multi-dimensional today. With present tuition centre being run successfully, more initiatives could be attempted to facilitate HCD.

The fact that no networking with other churches or NGOs was initiated by the mission as a policy drew attention for critical review. Collaboration and cooperation could bring more results. Lack of inter-dependency among missions and churches diluted effectiveness of witnessing.

Unit 2: Challenges to HCD and family

It was learnt that children grew in unhealthy family atmosphere in terms of spiritual, physical, cognitive and social development. That meant some steps must be taken in order to educate parents on these issues. That the mission did not initiate anything for this need shows that the mission lacks objective intervention.

Unit 3: Role of tuition centre in facilitating HCD

Since the goal was strictly to evangelise, there were no activities of facilitating HCD as such. The interviewee said that there was an annual training program for tutors and pastors. During such programs, HCD could be introduced.

Unit 4: Opportunities for and Challenges to mission

Tie up with the local church that was located inside the slum was advantageous for witnessing and mission. Tuition centre was used as a platform to evangelize children.

Chapter 11

Tuition Centre 3:
In Pursuit of Social Service

When I was told by the interviewee, "The church's only condition for children is that they must attend Sunday school on Saturdays in this same campus. Those who fail to fulfil this condition, we cannot allow them for tuition classes here," I was taken back. It seemed ironic that such a hard approach should be taken to lead the slum children to Jesus, the lover of children. As he noticed the frown on my face, he continued, "Otherwise, you know, they will simply grind chilli paste on our heads." This was a Tamil colloquial phrase to mean being fooled.

This tuition centre for the children from nearby slum Santosh Nagar was run in the campus by a century old mainline church. It belonged to a mainline denomination. It was commendable to see the voluntary tutors sitting with the children. Everyone followed weekly schedule to give time for children, some on Mondays, some on Tuesdays and others twice a week etc. These volunteers were retired teachers and some of them worked in schools. The Coordinator of the church tuition ministry was a retired officer from government department. He sat with me three times to complete the full process of discussion as per interview schedule.

Slum, Children and Families

There were about 2000 families living in Santosh Nagar slum along the railway track at the time of the research. Most of them lived in the five storied apartments built by Slum Clearance Board. Others lived in rows of houses separated by a street measuring not more than five feet in width. Men were employed either as auto rickshaw drivers or as load men in nearby Egmore railway station. Women worked as house maids. Conversation with the women indicated that vulnerability of the children falling into immoral trap is the biggest threat faced by parents.

Few tuition classes were run in the houses for children from classes 1 to 10. Tuition fee is collected. The fee varies depending on the classes. The children went to Muthaia Chettiar Tamil Medium School in Purasawalkam and Corporation School in Egmore. Some children attended Matriculation schools. Residents had access to Kilpauk Medical College Hospital, Rajiv Gandhi General Hospital and Egmore Children Hospital. There were no recreational facilities in the slum.

There was no church in the slum. About 10-15 families attended the Apostolic Christian Assembly (ACA) and other independent churches in other parts of Chennai. Evangelists from these churches visited the families and conducted prayer meetings where neighbours of other faiths come to the prayer meetings.

Tuition Centre

According to the pastor, the tuition centre rendered a social service to the neighbourhood. This tuition centre, called as Study Centre, had been functioning inside the church campus for the past ten years. Tuition classes were conducted in the evenings from 6pm to 7:30pm, five days a week, Monday to Friday. An escort was available to take the children back to their houses across the road with heavy traffic. 40 children from 4th class to 12th class were being benefited by this centre. Both boys and girls were admitted.

For want of space, more demand for admission could not be met at the time of the research.

Administration

A coordinator took care of the functioning of the centre. The church committee provided funds for the programs. 17 volunteers served as tutors. One of the tutors recollected that about 15 children of the slum who were in colleges or employed, were now practicing Christians. They preferred going to Tamil churches in Chennai because this church conducts services in English.

Purpose

This tuition centre served the purpose of reaching children and parents with the gospel by helping the children in their studies.

Child Friendly Environment

Good infrastructure like tables, chairs, toilets, and drinking water were available. Educational charts were displayed on the walls. Tutors were mostly women, who were shown to be more sensitive and compassionate towards the children. The campus of the church provided a favourable ambience for the children to play around.

Case Stories

Success Story

Maheswari came to the tuition centre when she was in 5th class. Her father died due to some illness. Her mother worked as a sweeper in an office. She passed 10th class with exceptionally good marks. For her Higher Secondary course (Plus Two), she joined one of the best schools for which a large amount of fee had to be paid. The church came forward to pay the fees. Maheswari is currently in her College final year. She has shared her testimony in the church. According to the interviewee, the reason behind Maheswari's success lies in her attending the tuition and Sunday Classes regularly and her ambition to develop. The spiritual nurture she received from Sunday classes and VBS formed in her a strong faith in Jesus Christ. It was seen that she overcame all her struggles with the support of faith and hard work.

The coordinator of the tuition centre involved in advocacy by meeting the school authorities to consider concession for a girl from a slum. She could pursue higher education only because of the financial support from the church.

Failure Story

Child Dinesh, came from an Odiya family that migrated to Chennai about 30 years ago. The family had five children. He had poor IQ but tremendous memory power. He regularly attended tuition and Sunday classes till he reached 12thclass. He further joined a college. However, in spite of much effort from the church and tuition centre, Dinesh could not succeed in life beyond the slum. He eventually ended up as a Coolie in Egmore railway station.

Educating Parents on HCD

Out of the 39 children in the centre, 36 came from Hindu families and 3 children from Christian families. Every year a parents' meet was organised in the church campus. Only mothers attended the meeting. They were counselled on HCD through a time of prayer and Word of God, and through addresses on issues of child care, health, social and economic development. A child who performed poorly in exams was expected to bring parents to the tuition centre for counselling on their role in supporting their child's development.

Every week the Outreach Team from the church visited the parents, mostly mothers, at their doors to pray, share the gospel and counsel. On invitation, parents gathered to witness their children performing in the final day program of VBS.

Spiritual Development

Challenges

Children were largely influenced by bad role models, especially fathers, who were commonly alcoholics and were known to perpetuate domestic violence. They exhibited religious piety by observing rituals like Ayyappa traditions. About 10% of children were said to join in the pilgrimage to Ayyappa shrine in Sabharimala, Kerala. This church being conducted in English, was not able to cater to the spiritual needs of children as children expected a Tamil service. Children were also found to be hesitant to join affluent families in the church. Factors like influence of anti-Christian political parties preventing children from going to church were found to challenge the spiritual development of children to some extent.

Monitoring

Any interest shown by the child in leading daily prayer time, memorising Bible verses, attending Sunday classes and VBS was observed.

Core Activities

Tuition started and closed with prayer that included recitation of the Lord's Prayer and Psalm 103:1-2. Every Saturday evening, children gathered for Tamil Sunday classes. Attending Sunday class was made compulsory. Every child in classes 6 and above was presented with a Bible every year. Bible Stories Comic Books were also provided.

Networking

Preachers are invited from outside for VBS valedictory program. No other resources from other ministries or missions are utilised for spiritual development of children.

Physical Development

Challenges

Children's health was affected by poor hygienic environment. There were no proper ventilation and sanitation in the houses. Children were not fed nutritious food. Buying food items from slum street vendors caused health problems.

Monitoring

No measures for health monitoring like height weight recording were undertaken. During Medical Camps children's health condition was checked.

Core Activities

Every day children were served snacks like buns and biscuits before tuition hours. After the Medical Camp, a follow up is done. Almost every day, tutors spent 5-10 minutes speaking to the children about personal hygiene practices. Tutors took effort to carry out individual counselling for both boys and girls to manage physical development issues like puberty, reproductive system, growth and attraction towards opposite sex.

Networking

No networking was implemented for educating children on physical development issues.

Cognitive Development

Challenges

Children did not have favourable environment at homes to work on homework and study. There were several cases of children who were poor in studies dropping out by peer pressure. On the whole, parents, though not educated, wanted their children to be educated and succeed in life but they are not able to help them. It was observed that average students were highly vulnerable to dropping out of school due to lack of motivation.

Monitoring

Marks registers were maintained in the tuition centre to monitor the status of children in school. Marks scored in midterm tests, quarterly and half yearly exams were recorded.

Core Activities

Tutor-children ratio was maintained at 1:5. Handwriting exercises were made compulsory on daily basis. Tests were conducted every day. Morning tuition classes at 6am were arranged for children in 9th class and above. Special classes for Mathematics, Science and English were conducted on Saturdays for needy children. Children were taken on educational excursions to museums, forts, railways and to planetariums.

Networking

A computer training program was organised through a voluntary group in Chennai during summer holidays. Chess Club members from Chennai visited the centre to teach children chess during holidays.

Social Development

Challenges

Immorality in families and community like family violence, street fights, addiction to alcohol and extra marital relationships influenced the children. Men wasting time and gambling become undesirable role models for the children.

Monitoring

Observing the countenance of children often reveal the problems in their lives. Sad looking children were identified and any change in their behaviour were observed by tutors. The revelation that children from slum behaved properly inside the church compound surprised some of the church people who were earlier not favourable for running a tuition centre for slum children inside the church compound.

Core Activities

Being let inside the aesthetic looking church compound brought a remarkable development in the social behaviour of the children. Children were allowed to run around and play inside the compound. This brought about in them a sense of self dignity and respect. Children came neatly dressed and tidy. Educational excursions provided an opportunity for the children to develop proper social behaviour and have ambitions for their future. Travel and food were arranged by the Church. Children learnt about discipline, value of family life and friendships from Sunday classes.

Networking

No networking was made use of for facilitating social development of children in the tuition centre.

Children's Participation

Generally, children had no opportunity to participate in the programs of tuition centre. They were not expected to contribute by way of expressing their opinions and organizing events.

Caring for Adolescents

Doctors from the church were invited to address the children on adolescence issues occasionally. Children who had passed out from the centre often visited the tuition centre to give their testimonies. Special meetings were organized for adolescent children as per the availability of resource persons.

Patriotism

Not much attention was given to patriotism.

Secular resources

No secular magazines or books were utilized in the tuition centre.

Critical Analysis

Unit 1: Purpose, implementation and resources

The purpose of the tuition centre was stated as evangelizing slum dwellers through educational assistance. The study showed that the church ardently implemented all the activities with respect to scoring good marks but other aspects of HCD were not scrupulously included. It was exemplary that members of the church volunteered to tutor the children. The local church met all the expenses related to running the centre. This was a good model for a self sustained tuition centre.

Unit 2: Challenges to HCD and family

It was understood from the study that family situations and community environment in the slum were not favourable for HCD. Expectation of children for a Tamil service was yet to be implemented. Annual mass counselling and weekly individual counselling served the purpose of educating parents on HCD.

Unit 3: Role of tuition centre in facilitating HCD

Children were said to have developed self discipline and dignified behaviour as they came into contact with the ambience of orderliness and beauty of the church compound. It was learnt from the study that due care was given to adolescent issues. However, there was a disparity in educating them on patriotism, utilising secular resources like children's periodicals both in English and Tamil. A lack of developing participatory skills in children by way of providing opportunities to organizing events was observed.

Unit 4: Opportunities and Challenges to mission

The study showed that tuition centre creates a rapport between the church and the community. Every child attended Sunday class without fail. Hence, the purpose of mission engagement was fulfilled through the tuition centre. However, the presence of an antichristian menace by political cadres to stop children coming to church tuition centre was sensed.

Chapter 12

Tuition Centre 4: Neighbourhood Outreach Mission

The tuition centre in Old Chetpat slum was run in a rented house block. The Coordinator was contacted over phone for permission to undertake the study. After going through the documents pertaining to the study, she arranged for my visits to the centre and for interactions with children and tutors. Children found it easy to come to the centre as the centre was situated in the street leading to the slum.

Slum, Children and Families

Old Chetpat slum was located on the northern banks of Cooum River in Chetpat. There were 1500 families living here at the time of the research. They earned their living through daily wages jobs. A few mothers worked as housemaids in the neighbourhood. Some were street vendors. Mothers were of the opinion that social evils are the major threats for the development of children. There were some fatherless children who needed support and security. A few young people from the slum ran a free tuition program in the slum. Children of this slum attended Chetpat Corporation School, Madras Christian College School, Vallal Sbhapathi Seva Sadan and Shenoy Nagar Corporation School. One Corporation hospital and a private clinic run by a philanthropic group named Temple Services met the need of medical care of the slum population. There was neither a park nor a playground nor a library in this slum. Some children went to the school grounds for play during the evening hours.

Churches, Government and NGO

Tamil Baptist Church, Roman Catholic Church and Marthoma Church are located in the area. A Pentecostal church is coming up. A youth ministry by the name Shalom Youth Fellowship met every week in the slum. Sunday Classes were conducted by an evangelist from outside. Gospel outreach ministries were regularly carried out by Pastors and Evangelists of several independent churches. About 50-70 families attended the Pentecostal churches outside their habitation. Children went to Sunday school programs in Tamil Baptist Church and Marthoma Church. A Temple administration near the slum provided milk to all slum children every day. It also offered vitamin tablets and meals on the days of religious festivals and family celebrations like birthdays and wedding days of its members. Apart from individual houses, Slum clearance department has provided multistoried housings. No NGO works among these families and children here.

Tuition Centre

The tuition centre was one of the first activities of the Neighbourhood Outreach Mission of the Chetpet Parish of the church under consideration. This centre has been run for the past two and half years for the benefit of children of Old Chetpat slum. It was located in the slum area. The tuition centre worked each evening from 4pm to 6pmfrom Monday to Saturday. Twenty-nine children from LKG to 8th Class were enrolled in the tuition centre. They were selected on the basis of economic disadvantages and their desire to study and improve themselves. This desire was often that of the parents, mainly the mothers.

According to the Pastor of the church, the tuition centre is run as Christ's Ministry. He saw this as an opportunity for the congregation to know more about the life and challenges of slum children.

Two graduate girls rendered their services as tutors for children studying in first standard and above. One woman was employed to take care of KG children. The Church committee looks into the needs of the centre periodically. One of the Core Committee members served as Coordinator for the tuition centre. Finance needs were met by the church.

The purpose of the tuition centre was to express the love of Christ through our services to the less advantaged sections of society, specifically by improving their educational opportunities.

Child Friendly Environment

The centre was run in a spacious hall where children had freedom to involve in activities like drawing and indoor games. Benches and desks were available and toilet facility was provided. Drinking water was brought by children. Two young graduate girls looked after the children in classes 1-8 and a child care woman took care of the KG children.

Case Stories

Success Story

Anand's mother brought him to this tuition centre two years ago. His family situation is vulnerable as his father does not go to any work making the family miserable. His mother works as a housemaid in nearby houses outside the slum. Anand was a dull student. He did not have too many friends as he was very shy. After joining the tuition centre, Anand began to improve in studies. He was accepted admission in Madras Christian College School, one of the best schools in Chennai aided by Government. Anand also has a circle of friends now. He was in 6th standard at the time of this study, and he was occasionally seen coming forward to mind the children in the tuition centre.

Main reason for the success is the constant efforts by the tutors to motivate Anand to have an optimistic worldview on life and use his God given capacity for his development.

The role of his mother in sending her son to school and the centre was another reason for the success story.

Failure Story

Kavitha, an 8th standard girl, was living with her grandparents and regularly attended the centre. Her father died few years ago and her mother worked as a sweeper in a fruits shop. Kavitha did not show interest in studies but had a talent in drawing. She loved playing in the streets with other children. In spite of several efforts by tutors, Kavitha was not able to get through her school exams.

It was found through a medical check-up that Kavitha had thyroid problem for which she took regular medication. Doctors opined that due to thyroid problems, the cognitive development of child could be impeded.

Educating Parents on HCD

It was found that there were 10Hindu families and 15Christian families that were benefitted by the tuition centre. Weekly visits to the families were made by a social worker from the church. Parents Meetings were convened once in six months to guide the parents in child rearing, education, solving family issues and savings. Only mothers attended the meetings.

Spiritual Development

Challenges

Some parents opposed children learning about Jesus Christ. Peer pressure was the prominent cause that challenged spiritual development of slum children. Youth standing at street corners bully church-going children. Ungodly behaviour of parents and neighbours add to the challenge to spiritual development.

Monitoring

Involvement of children in daily prayer time was observed. Attendance and behaviour in Sunday school, VBS and Children Camps were noted to follow the spiritual development of a child. Sometimes children came up with prayer requests and share testimonies during prayer time. Children interested in memorising Bible verses were considered as progressing in spiritual life. There was no documentation for this dimension of HCD.

Core Activities

Children were encouraged to participate in daily prayer time in the centre. They were given opportunity to recite memory verses. Bible contests were organized every month. Children attended Sunday school, VBS, Carols and Christmas Rally. Some of them participated in the activities like Christmas plays, dances and singing. Such opportunities enabled the children to hear the Word of God and know more about Jesus Christ. During family visits, the social worker prayed with parents and children. Prayers were upheld for the tuition centre in the Sunday service.

Networking

The Tamil Baptist Church contributed to the spiritual development of children in the tuition centre. During Talent Sundays and Children Retreats in TBC, children participated in the events like singing, elocution, debate, drawing and essay writing.

Physical Development

Challenges

Poverty was the main reason for many families' inability to feed children properly.

Parents did not have time to prepare healthy food as they go to work early morning and return late evening. Therefore, children bought food from street vendors that may not be hygienic. Most of the children took the mid-day meal in corporation schools which is not nutritious. Maggi noodles was extensively used for ready-made consumption but it was later banned by the Government.

Water supply was provided by the corporation on a daily basis through tankers at five locations in the slum. During summer, this system is was frequently interrupted, adding to the plight of the families. Public toilets were used by the community and the outlet is connected to Cooum river. It is important to note that the Cooum river bank was a breeding ground for mosquitoes, which caused a lot of diseases. There was no proper drainage system and the accumulation of waste contaminated the environment.

Monitoring

Any serious illness was recorded at the time of admission in the admission form.

Medical check-up results and weight measurement were documented every six months. Children were observed for symptoms of sickness during tuition hours and mothers were informed if necessary.

Core Activities

The tuition centre served snacks prepared with cereals and pulses every day. Once in six months de-worming tablets were given. For weak children, a health tonic was provided. A set of clothes and footwear were presented every year at Christmas. Children took part in the Annual Sports Day conducted by the church. Almost every day children were given awareness on health practices like hand washing, bathing, nail cutting, clean dresses and healthy food. During family visits, the social worker spoke to the parents and adolescents on the issues of sexual wellbeing.

Networking

For medical treatment, children were referred to doctors and the church met the financial needs for medical treatment.

Cognitive Development

Challenges

The overall environment of one room houses and quarrelsome parents was not conducive to studies. Those who failed in exams were so psychologically discouraged that they dropped out of school and looked for jobs. Girls were generally sent as housemaids in the neighbourhood or married off before the age of 18. Even studious children were not able to pursue college education due to the poor economic situation of the family.

Monitoring

Weekly and monthly tests were conducted and grades recorded. Copy of progress card from school is recorded for reference, and to check the need for special care for those weak in studies.

Core Activities

Every child was made to practice handwriting exercised and individual attention was given. Extra efforts were taken for weaker children in studies. Special coaching was given during exams. Saturdays were set apart for indoor games and fun activities like puzzles and riddles. The children were encouraged to prepare and speak on general topics.

Members of the church who worked as teachers visited the children twice a month to help in spoken English. Other members also visited occasionally to encourage the children in studies and help them improve in other subjects like Mathematics and Science.

The church was involved, on its own, in facilitating cognitive development of the children in the centre. There was an apprehension that letting in outsiders might give rise to more problems than benefits. Also, since it had not been the practice in the many years of its existence, the risk of new attempts was possibly not considered worthwhile.

Social Development

Challenges

Family situation, slum environment and peer pressures were the causes for the problems challenging social development of children. The children who were employed developed an attitude of self-sufficiency that leads to deviant behaviour with the mentality "Why should I be different from other slum folks?" These child labourers were able to earn money but they were not willing to improve their life through educational opportunities like Distance Education Scheme and Bridge School.

Monitoring

The personal care practises of children in the centre like combing properly, neat dressing, looking smart and cultured words were observed every day. Opinions from parents about child's behaviour in the family and from friends in school were noted down.

Core Activities

Regular counselling was given to the children on proper behaviour and developing self-dignity and self-control. On Saturdays, a social worker from the church talked to the children on developing good social life by self control, choosing good friends, obeying elders and keeping away from vices like stealing, lying, fighting, envy and greed. Moral teachings were given at times.

Networking

No other agencies from outside the church were involved in the activities for the social development of children in the tuition centre. The Tamil Baptist Church in the neighbourhood organized programs for children periodically. It proved helpful for the children in learning proper social behaviour and self development.

Children's Participation

Generally, children did not participate in contributing to organizing programs since they were considerably young in age. At times they asked for conducting special events like Sports Day and it would be organized.

Caring for Adolescents

This was not applicable to this tuition centre as children above age 12 were not enrolled. The church committee was aware about the practical issues related to dealing with adolescents. It was also understood that the present administrative capacity was not sufficient to handle adolescents, especially girls, from the slum. Parents of adolescent girls needed to be assured of the girls' security while they returned home from the tuition centre, which was quite late in the evening. The work load in the higher classes, was more than that of the lower classes which required them to stay late in the tuition centre. Taking into account such factors, the church tuition centre did not admit adolescent children.

Patriotism

On Independence Day and Republic Day, children delivered special addresses on topics like national leaders and freedom struggle. Snacks were distributed on such days.

Secular Resources

A Children's Library in the centre contained story books and general knowledge books like 'Genius' for children. No periodicals were provided in the centre.

Critical Analysis

Unit 1: Purpose, implementation and resource

The data reveals that the tuition centre was run by the church for the purpose of expressing the love of Christ in action by way of educational assistance. Activities were implemented in a well organized manner. The centre being run in the slum, in a rented building was an advantage both for witnessing and for the children to reach the centre safely. The study recognised the need of training the tutors periodically for serving the children holistically. This centre proved to be a good model of self sustained tuition program run by a local church without foreign fund.

Unit 2: Challenges to HCD and family

The study shows that the living environment, lack of parental care and poverty were the main challenges a child faced with respect to HCD. Regular visits to families and convening parents meetings by a social worker was a positive measure taken by the church.

Unit 3: Role of tuition centre in facilitating HCD

During the visits, the environment of the centre was observed to be child friendly. The study revealed that networking initiated with a neighbouring church was helpful in facilitating spiritual and social development of the children. Secular books for children were not used and this was identified as something that could be taken into consideration.

Unit 4: Opportunities and Challenges to mission

From the data, it was discovered that some parents reacted negatively to introducing Jesus Christ to the children. However, the fact that the centre continued to function in the slum itself testified for a favourable environment for mission.

Chapter 13

Conclusions, Reflections and Recommendations

The overall impression out of the study is that tuition centres are welcome by parents. They do not hesitate to send their children to tuition centres in the church compounds. This gesture of parents gives way for a favourable situation for the children to know Jesus Christ. It can be expected that these children would come to have faith in Jesus and develop spiritual life in the future when they become self supporting adults. Except for one tuition centre, leaders and staff of the other centres did not seem to be aware of HCD mission. Nonetheless, their commitment to teach Jesus to children cannot be undervalued.

It was evident that all the four agencies running tuition centres were devoted to bringing the children and families into the Church. While this seems to be the sole purpose of running the centres there is a danger that the spirit of evangelism may turn to be mere proselytizing. There is no doubt that tuition centres serve the purpose of communicating the love of God in Jesus Christ, however, we need to be cautious to not invite trouble of being accused of converting by alluring.

A table of comparison between the four tuition centres with respect to their role of facilitating HCD, in reference to objectives and factors, is given below:

Factors related to HCD	Tuition Centre 1	Tuition Centre 2	Tuition Centre 3	Tuition Centre 4
Purpose	Holistic Child Development	Transformation of People for Christ	Involvement of church in Social service	Neighbourhood mission
Implementation	Tuition centre is run through local church by International Child Development Organization	Tuition centre is run through local church by national Mission organization	Tuition centre is run by the church inside church campus	Tuition centre is run by local church in a hired apartment
Knowledge of HCD	Yes	No	No	No
Funding/ Sustain ability	Foreign Agency. No contribution from parents	Foreign as well as Indian funding	Church fund. No contribution from parents	Church fund. No contribution from parents.
Networking	Yes	No	Occasionally	No
Secular Resources	No	No	No	No
Participation of Parents	Yes	No	No	No
Participation of Children	Yes	Occasionally	No	No
Documentation of parameters regarding HCD	Yes	No	No	No
National Interest	No	No	No	No

From the observation of the table we can understand the disparities in facilitating HCD. What we have gained from the study of the four tuition centres reveals the similar and different approaches each centre takes to facilitate HCD. 'What they do not do' for HCD is also pointed out to some extent, but that does not come into the scope of this study. We can, on the whole, conclude that the committee and staff of the tuition centres, except the first one, are in need of the knowledge about HCD. Mostly they were not aware of the existence of one such mission dimension.

The following conclusions and recommendations can be made:

- Children in slums live at constant risk with respect to their spiritual, physical, cognitive and social development.

- The phenomenal growth of slums calls for mission engagement among children specifically. Since children encounter multidimensional challenges, the mission needs to be holistic. After all, God purports his mission to be holistic. In addition to evangelistic ministries, children need to be ministered holistically in order to see that they become Christ-like citizens in every sphere of life with spirituality at the core.

- For ministering to children living in vulnerable contexts of multidimensional challenges, the emerging mission concept of Holistic Child Development is so relevant that it is indispensable. The urgent duty of the Church is to do everything to educate pastors, leaders, missionaries, ministers and everyone connected with children ministry with the knowledge of HCD.

- Children are special and precious to God. Children have been used by God in the mission of salvation. It is God's mandate for parents and communities that children are developed holistically by tutoring them in the ways of God. Therefore, the Church and its mission are to give priority to tutoring children holistically.

- Education has been a well proven mission strategy for centuries which can be carried on today through tuition centres.

- Children in mission fields and the church's neighbourhood can be served effectively for their holistic development through tuition centres.

- Terms like "for Christ" and "outreach mission" may be avoided in the documents of missions. While there is a notion that such terms are helpful in getting foreign funds, it is often viewed with suspicion of mission trade. It is better to simply state 'Child development.' Likewise, 'Projects' might replace 'Missions' in the days to come.

- Care must be taken regarding implementation of tuition centres. Parents and community leaders can be consulted. This will also give them a sense of dignity and responsibility. Without community involvement HCD is incomplete.

- Dumping enormous money for initiating tuition centre is not necessary. Quality of time spent with children is most vital.

- Instead of asking the children to come to a location of our preference, it is advisable to go where the children and parents find convenient.

- Involvement of local churches in running tuition centres, without foreign support, will be exemplary and beneficial in several ways. It creates the right opinion of the Church among parents and the public. Such cooperation among Christians will be the most effective witnessing for the Lord.

- Networking is to be developed. Administrators of tuition centres of different denominations seldom exchange and share resources among one another. Forming an association of churches and missions running tuition centres will be highly profitable. Resources of both Christian and secular backgrounds can be utilised for HCD through networking.

- Non utilization of secular resources by the Church in general is a very serious concern these days. There are numerous books for children available in the market. They are stimulants for children particularly in their formative period to develop constructive world views. The Church must break the boundaries of orthodoxies that quarantine children inside the four walls of religion. Apart from gospel movies, films produced by Children Film Society can be screened. An attitude of Christian spirit and secular content is the need of the hour.

- Participation of children in running the tuition centre will pave a way for developing future leaders in the communities. Including children in discussions regarding activities in tuition centre will make them feel loved, accepted, respected and included.

- All the four tuition centres lack in the area of developing national interest in children. Children in their teens need to be educated about stark issues that curtail national development. Political, social, ecological, economical, technological aspects of nation building must have a place in HCD.

- The Church and its mission can consider tuition centres as a pioneering effort in mission to prepare the soil for sowing. A need is felt to develop a model tuition centre inculcating HCD.

A GO

Contextual and Transformational Tuition Centre

Chapter 14

Project Cycle Management (PCM): A Tool for Development Ministry

Project Cycle Management (PCM) is a tool used for organizing projects related to developmental interventions. Unlike welfare projects, developmental projects require systems of survey, need and capacity analysis, resources mapping of target people, goal setting and expected outcome. The concept of PCM provides principles and guidelines for applying in developmental projects. There are expert facilitators in this exercise who can be hired by churches and missions to have thorough training on PCM. Basically, PCM is a scientific method of arriving at decisions regarding need and nature of a project meant for developing communities. In this case, PCM can be adopted by churches and missions for organizing tuition centres also.

Scientific Methods for Missions

We know that spirituality is something beyond science. At the same time, spirituality need not negate science. Science is the study of any physical thing that is related to human life. And everything that is related to human life is created by God. This is the basic understanding of science in Christian spirit. Great inventors like Michael Faraday, Maxwell, Kelvin, and Fleming were all committed followers of Jesus Christ. So, if there is a scientific method for planning tuition centre and measuring development of children, then, why don't we adopt it? There exists such a tool called Project Cycle Management (PCM).

Principles of Development

Let us take the example of a child. In infancy it needs to be carried, then the child learns to walk with the help of holding someone or something. In few more months the child is able to stand on its own legs and walk. This is the progress generally found in a healthy normal child. It is not the end. One day the grown up adult can carry another child and help the child walk on its own. This is the ultimate goal of development.

Growth of a tree can be another example of development. It sustains itself. It multiplies on its own. Outside dependency is done away with in due course of time. Likewise, HCD is to result in self sustenance with respect to organizing and running any activity like tuition centres that facilitates HCD of next generation. The tuition centre in the village Puliur about 40 kms from Chennai was one among few centres organized by a Christian NGO 20 years ago. Now all the children have become young adults. It is overwhelming to know that these young adults help the next generation for education. This is the true impact of development. The following lines, taken from a famous quote, give the practical meaning of developmental ministry and we will do well in following these principles.

Go to people

Learn from them

Start from what they have

Show them how and encourage them to try themselves

Never do anything to make them feel "It's wonderful!" but to make them say, "It's workable!"

Educate, equip and empower

At the end the people will say, "We have done it by ourselves!"

This is the end success of a true social worker!

SMART Objectives

PCM employs objectives that are Specific, Measurable, Achievable, Realistic and Time bound. For a tuition centre, one of the objectives could be to see children who are scoring 20 marks to score 40 marks. Once the objective is set, the activities to achieve this are planned and once the activities are planned they are implemented. This exercise takes us in a direction with definite starting point and end point. We may change methods and means if necessary to reach the goal.

Components of PCM

PCM as a tool of developmental services commonly incorporates basic strategies of mobilization of people, consultation of people and participation of people. It is 'bottom to top' approach and not 'top to bottom.' In every phase of the development process the role of the target people or community or children and parents is central. Self Help Group (SHG) of women in villages is a classic example for PCM. PCM operates through four components. They are Base Line Survey, Project Designing, Implementation and Monitoring & Evaluation.

Diagram: Four Components of Project Cycle Management

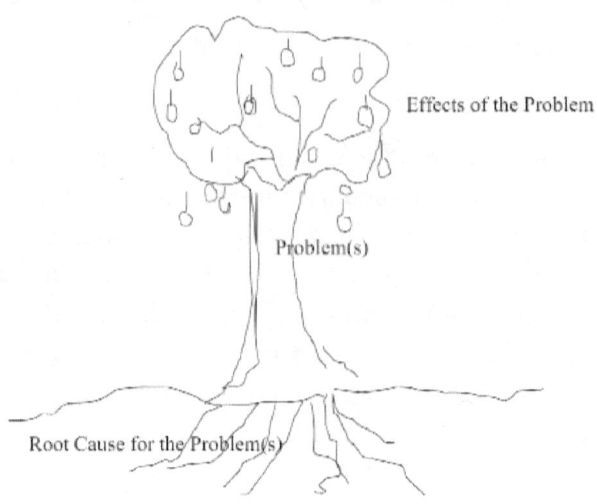

Diagram: Problem Tree to be evolved with participation of people

The purpose of Base Line Survey (BLS) is to know about the ground reality of the problem and available resources that can be utilised to solve the problem. Interviewing individuals and Participatory Rural Appraisal (PRA) are adopted for undertaking BLS. A Problem Tree and Resource mapping can be done in PRA. More than once, PRA may have to be convened. A diagram of Problem Tree above shows how this helps to arrive at crucial conclusions. Firstly, Problems are listed in the trunk part of the tree. Secondly, effects of the problems-Fruits are noted above the trunk. Finally, causes for the problem-Roots are listed. Focusing on causes of the problem will lead to considering various solutions that are specific, measurable, achievable, realistic and time bound.

Need/Capacity Analysis

Problem Tree exercise as part of PRA will lead to clarification about the problem and what possible interventions can be taken. Questions like 'Where can the project be implemented?' 'What is the exact need of the people?' 'What is the solution according to them?' 'What can they afford?' 'What are their capacities?' 'What resources are available?' can take us to the next component of Project Designing.

Project Design

Project Design involves three steps. Step one is writing down the list of activities that needs to be undertaken. Step two is budgeting. Step three is preparation of time chart. Activities and budget are finalized taking into account all the **inputs** necessary for carrying out the interventions so that the expected outcome is achieved. By 'inputs' we mean everything needed to deploy and employ, like human resources, infrastructures like buildings, and communication accessories etc., trainings for capacity building, transportations and finance. **Logical Frame Work (LFW)** can make the project effective since it provides several points of reference for implementing the project and for monitoring and evaluation. LFW has all the details of the project like objectives, expected outcome, means of verification, measurable indicators, risks and assumptions.

Budget includes every detail of fund mobilization and expenditures against all the activities planned. Annual budget can be divided into monthly, quarterly, half yearly and three quarter yearly budgets. Time chart shows which activities needs be undertaken on what period of weeks or months. Accordingly, this will be reflected in the budget. This will in turn forecast financial requirements in the time periods in which particular activities are to be implemented. Once the paper work is done, it takes us to the third component of PCM namely Implementation.

Project Implementation

This is the phase of the project that actually puts into practice all that has been worked out on the paper. Implementation involves day to day activities and periodical reviews. Reviews include both activities and finance positions. Changes are adopted when and where necessary as per new learning experiences. But the set objectives are to be strictly kept in view. Records, reports and references to changes are to be compared with Budget and LFW at review meetings. Documentation of activities, programs, progress, observations and meetings is vital.

Monitoring and Evaluation (M&E)

The process of monitoring and evaluation is necessary once in six months or one year. This process concerns program as well as finance. It can be carried out by going through records and reports in the administration section and by visiting the place of project in person to interact with people. This is generally done by an outsider. Remarks and recommendations of M&E are further used to make necessary improvements or alterations in the project design or implementation.

PCM makes a handy tool for organizing tuition centres in slums. Following the methods of PCM and holding on to all the details worked out on the paper will be helpful in making the tuition centre move towards the objectives of HCD.

PCM for Tuition Centres

If tuition centre ministry is seen as a 'project' then PCM is applicable to tuition centre ministry. Because it is our conviction that tuition centre ministry facilitates holistic development of children. When we say 'development' there should be a starting point and finishing point. In between, there is a process involved to move the project forward from starting point to finishing point. This is where PCM is found to be an appropriate tool for organizing the project of tuition centre ministry in terms of need/capacity analysis of children, objectives, expected outcome, and so on.

Chapter 15

Transformational
Tuition Centre of HCD Mission

In this chapter we will try to find a way for initiating tuition ministry. Growing slum population calls for our attention. Number of children being reached through existing tuition centres of missions and churches is very little that the challenge of reaching more children at risk stares at us. The question before us is: "How do we begin a tuition centre?" Before answering this, I would like to emphatically spell out one vital issue that every church and mission is much concerned about. That is, to lead children to Jesus Christ. If the parents are suspicious about the initiative and refuse to permit prayer in the centre, what can be done? If no Christian activity is allowed in the centre, will the church or mission be willing to start tuition ministry for the sake of children? As Christians, we have an incontestable mandate to follow Jesus in helping children unreservedly. Let India know the Jesus of unconditional love through our work. Following are a list of convictions:

- God loves every single child as each child is precious to God.

- God came into the world as a child and grew up holistically.

- It is God who has given the child to our care.

- Every child is unique and has its own life situation in family and community.

- God uses children and adults alike for HCD of each child.

First, God's leading is to be sought in finding a slum in need of tuition centre. Next, the idea of mission tuition centre must be announced in the church generally and discussed prayerfully in the committee. The church must be informed for prayer support and contributions of ideas and information. Consequently, a separate committee for the mission tuition centre could be organized. Required resources like tutors and sponsors should be identified in the church. If anyone in the slum is willing to be a tutor, it should be welcomed. Decide on how many children and of which classes could be accommodated in the centre and boys or girls or both. Make use of PCM guidance for collecting information from parents. This will help creating rapport with parents as well. Based on PCM documents, as explained in the previous chapter, activities and budget are to be prepared. The same can be presented to the committee for approval.

Develop Strategic Location

For deciding the place of the mission tuition centre, a direct visit to the slum and having informal conversation with the people in the slum and listening to their opinion would be helpful. Preference should be given to slums where some church members reside.

The venue of holistic tutoring need not be confined to one particular place like church compound. Jesus' holistic tutoring took place wherever people assembled to hear him. Centres inside slums are convenient for children to access to. Tutors' commitment to the HCD of the children would be seen by the whole community when the centre is located inside a slum. This can also avert the impression of conversion. Having the tuition centre in the slum or in the neighbourhood is advantageous for common visibility, easy accessibility and practical witness.

Create Child Friendly Environment

For a child-friendly environment, the tuition centre must be provided with desks and tables, spacious rooms, drawings, charts, and water and toilets. In many situations such facilities may not be feasible but a child-friendly tutor is all that matters. Availability of sufficient number of staff to give personal attention in all centres improves child friendliness. A child-friendly environment in a tuition centre enhances the child's enthusiasm to come to the centre. It helps develop a positive attitude of being in a safe and secure place with people who love and care for the child. One to one counselling must be arranged once a month. A child counsellor can be engaged for this service who will record important remarks, if any, that requires action. The staff must keep reminding the children to feel free to inform whenever they undergo verbal, physical, sexual or any other form of child abuse either by adults or any of the other children.

Often slum children face discriminative treatment in schools. Tuition centres should enable children to overcome this challenge. A caring and compassionate relationship between children and tutor in the centre matters more than environmental factors like infrastructure and facilities. One tutor for every 20 children should be an ideal ratio.

Initiate a Process of Documentation, Monitoring and Evaluation

Child psychologists and scientists have developed several indicators to measure HCD with respect to different age groups. These indicators can be used as standard of reference in general to ensure child's progress. Proper periodical documenting should be practiced in order to evaluate the outcome with reference to the standard ones. At the time of admission into tuition centre, every child must undergo an evaluation process that shows where the child stands with respect to HCD. Information obtained through fact finding process like enquiry, observations, oral and written tests at the time of admission must be recorded with date and names of persons involved in the process.

A Child Development Record in the form of file or register that contains sections allotted for each component of HCD must be maintained for each child separately. These findings are the Base Line Data. Base Line Data is the primary document or record by which the initial condition of a child at the time of admission into the tuition centre with respect to the four components of HCD is brought to the attention of the tutors and the manager or coordinator of tuition centre. Based on this information individual attention must be given to improve the status of the child with respect to HCD.

The evaluation process with respect to **spiritual development** should begin with an enquiry about the faith background of the family, the child's knowledge about Jesus Christ, child's participation in Sunday School or prayer meetings before, and willingness to know about Jesus Christ. Recording of indicators like child's participation in prayers, showing interest in Bible stories, attending church, Sunday school, spiritual programs like retreats and camps should be helpful in monitoring and evaluating spiritual development.

Regarding **physical development** enquiry must be made about past illness or medical treatment or physical inability of the child, and recorded. Children can undergo a medical check up by a doctor who will record his/her findings and recommend prescriptions. Body Mass Index that is calculated using height and weight of the child should be recorded and compared against standard chart. Any discrepancy found between actual and standard must be noted for remedial steps in consultation with doctor. Measuring height twice a year and weight every month should be helpful in monitoring health conditions. Updating of health record should be maintained for each child by entering information about illness and treatment. Such system should be helpful in monitoring health progress and taking preventive steps if needed.

In the case of **cognitive development** the standard of a child can be assessed by recording school progress report or conducting a simple test in the centre. This will provide information about the child's capacity in comprehending subjects and scoring marks. In addition to this, the child's inherent interests in skills like singing, drawing, reading, dance, sports, writing stories, poems, essays and playing musical instruments can be recorded to initiate evaluation of child's cognitive development. Continuous recording of information about the child's participation in contests and competitions in school or church will be a valuable indicator for assessing his/her cognitive development.

With respect to **social development,** the practice of evaluation and documentation could begin with observing the way the child exhibits self-awareness by keeping his/her head combed, face washed and being clean and dressed neatly. Knowing about the child's friends, hobbies and leisure activities should be helpful in assessing social inclinations of the child. Information about the child's behavioural indicators both positive and negative like friendliness, obedience, self-tidiness, attending to domestic chores, interest in group activities, respecting elders, anger, temperament, and responsibility towards school work can be obtained from parents and teachers.

Maintaining an attendance register that shows child's interest or disinterest in attending the tuition centre is the best practice of documentation to evaluate child's progress in social development. Observations of child's progress in terms of behaviour and participation in activities must be recorded periodically. Review meetings on weekly and monthly basis should be convened. Based on the documents maintained in the centre, development of each child must be monitored and the course of further intervention be planned to reach the goal of HCD.

Ensure Spiritual Development

Children in tuition centres come from Christian families as well as from other faiths. Children from Christian families can be encouraged and motivated to involve in spiritual activities like leading daily prayer and singing without any reservations. It need not be the case always that all children in the tuition centre attend the same church. Hence, denominational bias must be avoided. However, children from Christian families need spiritual nurture since most of the Christian families in slums are first generation believers and parents are not familiar with the Bible or are unable to read the Bible themselves.

In the case of children of other faiths, care must be taken not to practice any coercion. Parents are understandably apprehensive of cultural and identity losses caused by popular Christianity. Children who do not show interest in spiritual activities can be counselled lovingly. In the event of evangelistic programs, it is safer to ensure that the children attend such programs only with the consent of parents. Care must be taken not to criticize or stop children's participating in religious activities of other faiths in their families. No discrimination should be shown between children involved in spiritual activities and those who do not. Each child and the family must be prayed for using a name list of children in the church. It must be remembered that spiritual growth needs the working of the Holy Spirit and witnessing life of everyone involved in the ministry.

Ensure Physical Development

Physical body of children certainly constitutes a part of God's image. Hence, tuition centres must take particular care of this aspect of HCD. As mentioned earlier, periodic recording of Body Mass Index of children by measuring height and weight is to be followed. A self-hygiene register can be maintained to check habits like nail cutting. In case of adolescent children a curriculum can be developed for educating them on sexuality and self-hygiene.

A health register can be kept for recording any illness of every child. This arrangement should help study the frequency of illness in order to take necessary action. Organizing health screening camps periodically should be helpful in preventing serious health issues. NGOs and hospitals organizing free medical camps can be approached for this purpose.

Slum living keeps children highly vulnerable to physical harm in terms of poor housing and sanitation, seasonal health threats, stressful family environment, poor food intake, superstition and gender discrimination. Tuition centres must organize programs to create awareness among children and parents to prevent accidents and diseases.

Ensure Cognitive Development

Cognitive development of slum children is affected by their family, community and school environments. Tuition centres must do the needful to ensure cognitive development of the children. Activities for cognitive development can be categorized under two broad themes: curricular and extra-curricular. Regarding curricular activity the first and foremost activity in the tuition centre should be assisting children to complete their home work. These children do not get adequate assistance from parents or teachers in schools. Moreover, they often experience a negative influence on their education from family, community and peers. In this context, children who are not able to complete the task of homework must be given individual attention in consultation with class teachers in school. The tutor should be able to devote extra time for such children. Conducting weekly tests in subjects should be helpful for the children to get more familiar with the practice of writing and finishing in time.

Stories and illustrations are found to be an effective catalysts in enhancing mental capacity to learn and understand. Jesus adopted this method. Narrating stories and providing story books and general knowledge books for children would enhance their skill of reading and comprehending. Collection of used books from church members and friends should serve the purpose.

Regarding extra-curricular activities, a time of quiz program in the centre every week can enhance their general knowledge. Newspapers and secular books published for children must be made available in the tuition centre. Such materials can be collected from friends and neighbours, free of cost. Children need to be provided with opportunities like music classes, clay modelling, drawing and indoor games, like chess, to exhibit and develop skills of creativity. Children must be encouraged to make picture albums and other handicrafts that can be displayed in the centre.

An annual educational excursion to nearby historical locations like forts, palaces, museums and monuments of national leaders would be helpful in improving their knowledge of the world around them. Slum parents are willing to do their best for their children's education. Parents can, therefore, be involved to meet the travel needs and provide food packets for their children. Talented children can be encouraged to participate in contests like drawing, essay writing, elocution and quiz conducted in schools and NGOs. Assistance to prepare for such events must be offered by way of providing books, coaching and mentoring. Expenses for this can be met through arranging sponsorship from church or friends.

Ensure Social Development

Every child is unique in the creation of God. A curriculum for children particularly in adolescence can be of great use for educating them on self control, cultivating respectable behaviours, developing positive attitudes, goal setting, stress management, and handling attraction towards opposite sex can be made available in the centre. Storytelling can help in building life coping skills in children. Tuition centres can see that children are taught to read books to grow in general knowledge and positive attitude. It is common that Christians do not look at secular books because they think that it will impair their spiritual growth. This stigma needs to end.

When we aim at HCD we must see that children have access to resources for their total development with regard to their spirituality and faith formation, character and conduct, knowledge and skills, attitude and world view. A time can be fixed when children are allowed to spend time on reading books and watching children's movies. Children must be taught to choose good things in their surroundings for the world is filled with both good and evil.

Social development of children in slums can be ensured when these children grow in dignity. In general, slum children are influenced by the culture of poverty, oppression and negative world views. Tutors and others must treat them in the way that assures them that they are respected. Birthdays of children can be celebrated in the centre. Appreciation before others will enhance their self esteem. It is better to avoid reprimanding them in front of others especially in the case of adolescents. Regular consultation with professional counsellors will be helpful in facilitating social development of children.

Develop a System for Parents' Care

Tuition centres must attempt to guide parents in their task of bringing up their children. Giving them the hope of moral support can be valuable. Parental supervision in bringing up children in terms of spiritual, physical, cognitive and social developments should not be undermined. Periodic meetings with parents will be helpful where they can learn about believing and following Jesus Christ, family maintenance, family planning, child rearing, sanitation, hygiene, communal harmony, income generation and savings. Since slum parents mostly work in unorganized sectors like construction sites and roadside shops they can be linked to government welfare schemes available for unorganized labours. They can also be linked to banks, post offices and insurance companies for small savings and insurance policies. Awareness programs on such schemes can be arranged by contacting the concerned government officials or NGOs.

Avail Resources for Capacity Building

Theological understanding of HCD, stages of child development and teaching of religions on various themes of HCD are especially relevant to the tuition centres. They further lead to the realization that capacity building of tutors, mission leaders and church leaders is the need of the hour. Children's developmental issues vary depending on stages of growth and family environments. For providing holistic care, the staffs of tuition centre and church committee need to undergo periodical training to improve their knowledge on developmental issues of children in different age groups. Children from families of other faiths would find many differences between the teaching of the Bible in the tuition centre and religious practices of their parents and relatives. Tutors when educated on theological perspectives of mission in multi-faith context should be able to help those children overcome the dilemma.

Church's lack of knowledge on relevance of mission to poverty and HCD constitutes one of the challenges to HCD in slum context. Gaining knowledge on how poverty and family crisis affect the learning capacity of children should be helpful in understanding children who are weak in studies, and would also help in coping with the need of painful efforts in assisting such children patiently. Learning about the influence of family and community of slums on the behaviour and attitude of children should help the tutors to treat the children with empathy despite their disrespect, inability to avoid bad friendships, lack of punctuality, dishonesty and hostility towards development and learning about God.

Capacity building of staff and coordinating committee is necessary in updating knowledge on government schemes and NGOs related to development of slum families and children. The staffs need to be trained on the upkeep of documentation with respect to all dimensions of HCD. Existing NGOs can be of relevant help for exposure visits and trainings.

Encourage and Ensure Child Participation

Convention on the Rights of the Child of United Nations advocates ensuring the participation right of children. This aims at developing them to be respectable and responsible adults. Participation means having a say in planning, implementing and evaluating. A children's committee can be formed to take care of cleaning the centre and planning events like the celebration of national days, festivals and outings. Children can be asked how they would like to celebrate or what kind of snacks they would prefer. For instance, children can be consulted where they would like to go for a picnic program. Forming a Children Cultural Team that performs skits and musical items would be encouraging for the children. Children must be encouraged to collect old newspapers that contain supplementary books for children from their neighbourhood and distribute among other children in the centre.

Create Conscious Networking

To facilitate HCD, networking is necessary. Slum children face multi-dimensional challenges. In that case churches and missions must be willing to be transparent and share resources. It is disheartening to note that very few missions or churches are willing to work together. Recognizing others' skills and utilizing them will be helpful in addressing several needs of slum children. Slum children need help to access information and knowledge resources that support HCD. The Church needs to identify teachers, doctors, and trainers of music, games, handicrafts, and arts, to give their time for slum children. This can be made possible in three ways. First, resource persons within the church congregation can be mobilized. Normally, church members are more interested in preaching gospel and other related activities. They need to be reminded that God expects his Church to care for the needy holistically.

Second, resource persons from other denominations can be utilized. There is a barrier in between denominations that needs to be broken in order to serve one another in the name of Jesus

Christ who is common Saviour and Lord to all denominations. Third, resource persons from people of other faiths can also be made use of. Experts in the field of education, health, skill development, counselling, career development, family wellbeing, child rearing and social security are accessible. They can be utilized in the tuition centres.

Ensure Sustainability Factor

Non-dependence on foreign funds is one of the major mission challenges. It deters local congregation from being involved in the tuition centre ministry. Moreover, it propagates a message that foreign hand is behind the running of tuition centres, thus creating a suspicious attitude among public that Christians are 'foreign agents' being paid for 'conversion target'. Encouraging financial support of local congregations should be helpful for effective communication of gospel. In the case of setting up more centres in the future, more resources will be needed. Due to the increasing need for caring for HCD of slum children in the years to come, it is essential to find a solution for the problem of sustainability. Children who pass out from the centres and are employed can be encouraged to support the program. More volunteers could be mobilized. Activities could be planned with minimum or no financial encumbrances. Reliable Christians can be identified and mobilized as a team. This team in due course may take over running of the tuition centre.

Conclusion

In the backdrop of multidimensional challenges to HCD of slum children, tuition centres are found to be a relevant mission model for the Church and missions. God has blessed his Church with "numerous gifts of Spirit" (1 Corinthians 12). Resources in churches are unutilized or underutilized or wrongly utilized. This should be tapped and directed towards tutoring children unconditionally. Tuition centres can serve the purpose of facilitating HCD effectively, HCD being the relevant mission among children at risk in various contexts. The Church can quietly, humbly, indigenously and unconditionally serve children everywhere through tuition centres. A further need for research on running tuition centres in several contexts with the focus of HCD should be encouraged.

We live in a time of prevailing apprehensions regarding future of missions nationwide, but we have the great sovereign God of all times who has a Mission. So, let the Church pursue its mission and ministry for children in vulnerable life situations with the compassion of our Lord Jesus. When the Lord saw people, he was filled with compassion (Matthew 9:36). To this end tuition centres are worth all the efforts. For we know for certain that God can raise Christ-like leaders for the Church and the nation as well, through tuition ministry.

Bibliography

1.   ARTICLES IN JOURNALS

Kakoti, Gopal. "Status of Rural Migration-Need and Development Initiatives." *Kurukshetra: A Journal on Rural Development* Vol.62, No.11 (2014): 14-17.

Maliekal, Joy. "Shelter for the Urban Poor in India." *Religion and Society* 45(1) (1998): 104-110.

Manjaly, Thomas. "Social Responsibility: Jesus' Jubilee Message-Biblical Orientations and Pastoral Implication." *Indian Theological Journal* Vol.5, No.1&2 (2011): 3-43.

Shanmugavelayutham, K. "Child Care Services and the Urban Poor." *Religion and Society* 46 (3) (1999): 122-135.

Slimbach, Richard. "Learning from Slums: Study and Service in Solidarity with The World's Urban Poor." *Journal of Missiological Reflection,* Vol. IV. (2010): 126-151.

Thangaraj, P. "Sitrur Thirusabai Pudhumalarchi Thiruppani Samuga Samaya Arasial Poruladhara Nokkil (Village Church Transformation Mission in Social Religious Political and Economical Perspectives)." *IRAYIAL MALAR TTS* Vol.34 No.04 (October-December 2000): 24-25.

2.   ARTICLES IN PERIODICALS

Ahmed, Jacob. "Education and Jesus," *Light of Life*. Vol.59 No.04 April 2016. 31-33.

Ailawadi, Sanjiv. "Stories of our streets," *AIM*. Vol. 42 No.12. December 2013. 17-21.

Chandrababu, Divya. "Private children's homes in TN aided by corrupt system: Parents Lured Into Sending Kids With The Promise Of Better Future." *Times of India*. Chennai edn. 17 September 2014. 2.

______. "Race to finish lessons leaves students behind." *Times of India*. Chennai edn. 17 September 2014. 2.

Editorial. "Teaching in Govt Schools a Matter of Concern." *The New Indian Express*. Bengaluru edn. 15 January 2015. 10.

Mishra, Ambreesh. "Children at Work." *India Today*. 02 February 2009. 11-13.

Ramachandran, Smriti Kak. "Urban Housing Schemes at Slow Pace: Panel." *The Hindu*. Chennai edn. 21 December 2014. 12.

Sumi, H. Ilkuto. "Ecological Consciousness: Jesus Christ the servant-leader and the concern in minimizing environmental degradation." *The Answer: The Voice of the Indigenous Missions in India, Vol. 31 No.2 Sep 2015- Feb 2016*. 10-11.

Vaithyalingam, Ranjit. "Slum Kid Journalists," *Pudiya Thalaimurai*. Tamil Weekly. 04 September 2014. p. 46-47.

Rathi, Sujaya, Mohammad and Deebapriya. "Are Slums a Problem or Solution?" *The Hindu: Open Page*. Chennai edn. 12 July 2013. 12.

Raqshan, Tuba. "Relocation of slum-dwellers leads to sharp rise in dropout rates: Study." *dt NEXT Daily Thanthi*. Chennai edn. 23 March 2016. 1.

3.   BOOKS

Ahuja, Ram. *Social Problems in India*. 2nd edn. Jaipur: Rawat Publications, 1997.

Arles, Siga and others (eds). *Now & Next: A Compendium of Papers Presented at the 'Now & Next' Theological Conference on Children, Nairobi, Kenya*. Bangalore: CFCC, 2011.

Bakshi, Indu. *Understanding Children and their Problems*. Mumbai: Vakils, FEFFERS and SIMONS Ltd, 1997.

Battacharya, B. *Urbanization, Urban Sustainability and the Future of Cities*. New Delhi: Concept Publishing Company Pvt. Ltd., 2010.

Bharati, Dayanand. *Living Water and Indian Bowl*. Delhi: ISPCK, 2004.

BNB Publications. *What about the Slums: Connecting Gospel with Urban Underprivileged Families*. Mumbai: BNB Publications, 2006.

Borland, Moira and Others. *Middle Childhood: The perspectives of children and parents*. London: Jessica Kingsley Publication, 1998.

Bosch, David J. *Transforming Mission: Paradigm Shifts in Theology of Mission*. Bangalore: CFCC, 2006.

Brewster, Dan. *Child, Church and Mission: A Resource Book for Christian Child Development Workers*. Malaysia: Compassion, 2005.

________. *Biblical Themes on Children and Childhood in the Bible: Supplementary Guide*. California: Compassion International, 2007.

Brewster, Dan and Jesudason Jeyaraj. *Churches, Kingdom of God and Children*. Bangalore: GA-HCD Compassion International South Asia Unit, 2013.

Bush, Luis. *The 4/14 Window: Raising Up a New Generation to Transform the World*. Canada: Compassion, 2009.

Daniel, Brigid, Sally Wassel and Robbie Gilligan. *Child Development: For Child Care and Protection Workers*. London: Jessica Kingsley Publishers, 2010.

Davies, John Keith. *The Local Church: A Living Body*. Great Britain: CPD Wales, 1996.

Duncan, Michael. *Costly Mission: Following Christ into the Slums*. California: MARC-WV, 1996.

Gnanakan, Ken. *The Whole Gospel of God*. Bangalore: TBT, 2014.

Hopper, W.A.F. *Jesus: Master Educator*. Hyderabad: ETF Publication Trust, 2005.

Ingham, Kenneth. *Reformers in India: 1793-1833: An Account of the work of Christian Missionaries on behalf of Social Reform*. London: Syndics of the Cambridge University Press, 1956.

Ingleby, J.C. *Missionaries, Education and India: Issues in Protestant Missionary Education in the Long Nineteenth Century*. Delhi: ISPCK. 2011.

Jayakumar, Samuel. *Mission Reader: Historical Models of Holistic Mission in the Indian Context*. Delhi: ISPCK/ Oxford: Regnum International, 2002.

Jeyaraj, Jesudason Baskar. *Biblical Perspectives on Children and their Protection: Towards a Child Theology*. Madurai, Tamil Nadu: Jubilee Institute, 2007.

Lim-Tan, Rosalind. *Child Development & Functioning in Families and Communities*. Malaysia: HCDI, 2009.

Manoharan, J.N. *Christ and Children: Transformation of Next Generation*. Hyderabad: GS Books. 2017.

Manoharan, J N. *Christ and Cities: Transformation of Urban Centers*. Chennai: MEB, 2005.

Manoharan, Moses N. *Church: Towards Understanding Mission and Witness*. Chennai: ICSA/ Delhi: ISPCK, 2002.

Masih, Jonathan. *Contribution of Missionaries Towards Education in India*. Delhi: ISPCK, 2015.

May, Scottie and others. *Children Matter: Celebrating Their Place in the Church, Family, and Community*. Grand Rapids: Eerdmans, 2005.

Meinzen, Luther W. *A Church in Mission: Identity and Purpose in India*. Vaniyambadi: IELC Concordia Press, 1981.

Mohapatra, Samapika. *Exploring Slum Children' Life – World*. New Delhi: Serials Publication, 2012.

Myers, Bryant L. *Walking with the Poor*. New York: World Vision ORBIS Books, 1999.

Nambiar,K.K.Vijayan. *Psychology of Learning & Instruction*. New Delhi/Hyderabad: Neelkamal Publications Pvt. Ltd., 2004.

Nangia, Sudesh, and Sukhadeo Thorat. *Slum in a Metropolis: A Living Environment.* Delhi: Shirpa Publication, 2000.

Nath, Nibedita. *Growing Up in Slums.* New Delhi: Manak Publications, 2008.

Paulus, Vimala. *Introducing Christian Education.* 2nd edn. Bangalore: CSICCC, 1993.

Prabakar, Samson (ed). *Mission in the Past and Present: Challenges and Perspectives.* Bangalore: BTESSC/SATHRI, 2006.

Prince, Derek. *Who Cares for Orphans, Widows, The Poor and Oppressed? God does. Do we?* New Zealand: Derek Prince Ministries, 2000.

Rajaratnam, K. *Towards a Just Society: Church & Poverty: Paper Presented in Lutheran World Assembly, Hong Kong, July 1997.* Chennai: GTCRI, 1997.

Sider, Ronald J. *Good News and Good Works: A Theology for the Whole Gospel.* Michigan: Baker Book, 1999.

Singh, S.D. and K.P. Pothen, *Slum Children of India.* New Delhi: Deep & Deep Publications, 1982.

Vijayalakshmi, D. *Urban Poverty in Chennai City: A Study.* Chennai: Today Publication, 2009.

White, Keith J. *Introducing Child Theology: Theological Foundations for Holistic Child Development.* Malaysia: Malaysia Baptist Theological Seminary, 2010.

Yohannan K.P. *No Longer A Slumdog.* Carrolton: GFA Books, 2011.

Zuck, Roy B. *Precious in His Sight: Childhood and Children in the Bible.* Grand Rapids: Baker Books. 1996.

4.   ARTICLES IN BOOKS

Aghamkar, Atul. "Forming Christian Communities Among the Urban Poor," in Sebastian C.H. Kim and Krickwin C. Marak (eds), *Good News To The Poor: The Challenge to the Church.* Pune: CMS/ Delhi: ISPCK, 1997.

Arles, Siga. "The Contribution of Christian Nationalism to India's Development," in C.V. Matthew (ed), *Integral Mission: The Way Forward.* Tiruvalla, Kerala: Christava Sahitya Samiti, 2006.

_______. "Theological Education in India," in Siga Arles and Gnanaraj D. (eds), *Towards Indigenous Missions and Theological Education.* Bangalore: CFCC, 2012.

Arulmani, J.D. "Introducing Ourselves to Holistic Education," in Siga Arles (ed), *Called To Teach.* Bangalore: CFCC, 2011.

Athyal, Sakhi. "Spiritual Development of Children," in Jesudason Baskar Jeyaraj and others (eds), *Holistic Child Development Vol.1: Foundation, Theory and Practice.* Delhi; ISPCK /Bangalore: CFCD, 2013.

Balasundaram, Franklyn J. "The Dalits and the Christian Mission in the Tamil Country," in F. Hrangkhuma (ed), *Christianity in India*. Delhi: ISPCK/ Pune: CMS, 1998.

Benson, Warren S. "Christ the Master Teacher," in Robert E. Clark, Lin Johnson and Allyn K. Sloat (eds), *Christian Education: Foundations for the future*. Chicago: Moody Press, 1991.

Brewster, Dan. "Themes and Implications of Holistic Child Development Programming in Seminaries," in Jesudason Jeyaraj and others (eds), *Children at Risk: Issues and Challenges*. Bangalore: CFCD/ Delhi: ISPCK, 2009.

Budiardjo, Tri. "Creating God's Intended World for Children: A Biblical Reflection on the Reality of Children's world," in Jesudason Jeyaraj and others (eds), Repairer of Broken Walls: Essays on Holistic child Development: In honour of Dr. Dan Brewster. Delhi: ISPCK/ Bangalore: CFCD, 2014.

Christdhas, Abraham. "Religious Perspectives and Child Development," in Jeyaraj and others (eds), *Holistic Child Development Vol.1*. Delhi: ISPCK/ Bangalore: CFCD. 2013.

Daniel, Christina. "Gender Dimensions in Slums," in John Desrochers (ed), *India's Growing Slums*. Bangalore: Centre for Social Action, 2000.

George, Annie. "Child Theology in Holistic Child Development," in Thomas Swaroop (comp), *Child Theology and Holistic Child Development*. Bangalore: Compassion, 2011.

Gnanakan, Ken. "Jesus Christ and God's Whole Mission," in Paul Mohan Raj (ed), *Mission: Yesterday, Today, Tomorrow*. Bangalore: TBT, 2009.

Houghton, Graham. "The Foundation Laid by Christian Missionaries Towards Nation Building," in Ezra Sargunam (ed), *Christian Contribution to Nation Building* (Chennai: MEB, 2006).

Miles, Glenn. "Caring in Society," in Douglas McConnell, Jennifer Orona and Paul Stockley (eds), *Understanding God's Heart for Children: Towards a Biblical Framework*, Colorado Springs: Authentic/ London: Authentic/ Hyderabad: World Vision, 2007.

Penzel, Ute. "Child Rights and Church Boarding Homes," in Meshack (ed), *Child Rights: A Theological Exploration*. Chennai: GLTC, 2011.

Ribeiro, E.F.N. "Planning for the Urban Poor: Basic Needs and Priorities," in Alfred de Souza (ed), *Urban Growth and Urban Planning: Political Context and People's Priorities*. New Delhi: Indian Social Institute, 1983.

5.   INTERNET

http://www.righttoeducation/mhrd.gov.in

http:// www.unicef.org

http://www.hcd-alliance.org

http://www.compassion.com

http://www.worldvisionindia.com

hcd.institute@gmail.com

Interview Schedule
for Study of Select Tuition Centres

To Analyse Role of Tuition Centres
for HCD of Children in Chennai Slums

Respondents: Manager or Coordinator of Tuition Centres

General information about the Tuition Centre with respect to HCD

1. What is the purpose of starting the tuition centre?

2. What measures do you undertake to keep the tuition centre child-friendly?

3. According to your experience can you provide one success case story for learning purpose? It can be the development of a child spiritually, physically, cognitively and socially. Or if not in all, at least in some of these components. In other word the success story of a child for whom the tuition centre was helpful in overcoming obstacles to HCD. What do you think are the reasons for the success?

4. Can you narrate one failure case story of a child, if any at all, who, in spite of your interventions, was not able to come up

to your expectations in terms of HCD or in terms of some of the components of HCD? What is in your opinion the reason for the unsuccessful result? (Non cooperation of parents, lack of skills or capacity of tuition staff, influences of peer, health issues and any other reasons).

Place of Family in HCD

5. How does your tuition centre help parents to contribute to HCD?

6. What is the number of children in tuition program based on religious practices as given below?

Religious practice	Number of children
Goes to Temples	
Goes to Church	
Goes to Mosque	
Any other religious place	

Information on Children Development Activities

7. **Spiritual Development**

   Awareness

   a. What are the causes, in your perception, for the problems children of age 6-14 undergo that formulate their spiritual development?

   b. How do you monitor a child's spiritual development? (this question aims at finding out information on documentation practice of the centre)

Intervention

Internal Activities

c.   What are the measures taken by you to facilitate the spiritual development of children?

Networking

d.   How do you network with local churches and other Christian ministries for the spiritual development of the children?

8.   **Physical Development**

Awareness

a.   What are the common causes, in your opinion, for the problems slum children have with respect to their physical development?

b.   How do you monitor the physical development of the children? (this question aims at finding out documentation practice of the centre)

Intervention

Internal Activities

c.   What are the efforts taken by you to ensure the physical development of children in the age group of 6-14 with respect to self- hygiene, food habits and preventive health practice. What are the problems faced by you to achieve this?

d.   How do you help early adolescents (12-14), both boys and girls, manage physical development issues like puberty, reproduction system growth and attraction towards opposite sex?

Networking

e.   How do you involve local churches and other Christian and secular NGOs and government agencies for facilitating the physical development of children?

9.   Cognitive Development

Awareness

a.   What are the causes, in your perception, for the problems of children that challenge their cognitive development? (School drop-out, lack of motivation, child marriage, migration, poor performance in exams etc.)

b.   How do you monitor a child's cognitive development? (this question aims at finding out documentation practice of the centre)

Intervention

Internal Activities

c.   How do you facilitate the cognitive development of children in the age group of 6-14 with respect to education, general knowledge and talents?

Networking

d.   How do you network with local churches, schools and other agencies for the cognitive development of children?

10.   Social Development

Awareness

a.   What are the causes for the problems that children, in your opinion, of age 6-14 undergo that challenge their social development?

b. How do you identify issues and monitor social development? (this question aims at finding out documentation practices of the centre)

Intervention

Internal Activities

c. How do you facilitate social development of children with respect to self tidiness, hospitality, discipline, family, friends etc.?

d. How do you facilitate participation of the children in tuition program?

e. How do you impart life coping skills of social behaviour, goal setting, stress management, optimism, self control, gender equality and problem solving in adolescent children of age 12-14?

f. How does your tuition centre contribute to children towards patriotism?

g. How are secular resources like newspapers, children's books and periodicals helpful in facilitating HCD?

Networking

h. How do you network with local churches and other agencies for the social development of children?

Premparivar Tuition Centres in-Odisha

Prem Parivar tuition centres have been run in Odisha since 2010 by Faith Good Works Fellowship (FGF), a Christian Child Development Organization from Chennai. The author serves as Honorary Director. FGF came into existence after Christian persecutions of Khandhamal disrict, Odisha in 2008. **Happy Family and Communal Harmony** is the vision of FGF. The mission is community based HCD. The three-fold goal is to serve poor children in Odisha, to mobilise resources from Tamil Nadu and to develop leaders in Odisha. For more information the website can be accessed www.fgf-india.org

Tuition centre is the core activity of FGF. At present, tuition centres are run for the benefit of children of Ghasi community in Nineteen villages of Harbanga block in Boudh district. Ghasi community, coming under SC category, is the most discriminated community in this region. These children go to nearby government schools where they are often made to sit separately in classrooms.

Initiation

Mission workers meet the parents to get their cooperation to start a tuition centre. It is their responsibility to provide a place for the centre. In some instances, community room is offered for this purpose. Otherwise, the children sit on the ground under a tree or on the street. Children from 1-5 classes are admitted into the tuition centres. Each child gives two rupee as monthly fees. A volunteer from the community is appointed as Voluntary Tutor. He/she is expected to have completed at least class 8. A minimum monthly honorarium is offered for the service of tutorship.

Cognitive Development Services

A seven lesson curriculum is followed. It includes basic languages of Odiya, Hindi and English, basic Mathematics and life lessons. Basic language lessons help children to read and write alphabets, one letter words to four letter words and simple sentences. Basic Mathematics lesson aims at training children in addition, subtraction, multiplication and division. Life lessons contains themes like Education, God, Faith, Family, Hygiene, Discipline, Skill development, Social responsibility and Patriotism.

FGF provides school note books and bags to children for a token payment of Rs.10. Free text books up to class 5 are provided by the Odisha Government. Children Book Club has been organized in three villages. Books on general knowledge and stories are kept on request by the youth and children in the community.

Social Development Services

Annual Camps are held in villages. Child evangelists from Odiya churches are invited to teach games, choruses and moral values through stories. Special lunch is provided for which parents give hands to cook and serve.

Play items like balls, dolls, skipping ropes and cricket sets are collected from Christian families in Tamil Nadu, by way of money or materials, and distributed. National days are celebrated by organizing meetings where children sing patriotic songs, render speech and receive toffees.

Utilizing Secular Resources

Daily newspaper is circulated among these children. Children Book Clubs function in the centres. As per the choices of the children, books on general knowledge and fiction are kept in the collections. Every month a general moral story is printed in Odiya and distributed among the children.

Patriotism

Special events of singing, elocution and drawing are conducted on the eve of national days like Republic Day and Independence Day. Themes like Freedom Fighters, Independence Struggles and Patriotism are suggested for the contests for which prizes are presented to the children.

Physical Development Services

Once a week each child is given an egg for Rs. 1. Medical help by way of doctor fees and purchase of medicine is provided in part. Footwear is provided once a year.

Children participate in sports events. Old clothes are collected from Tamil Nadu and distributed. Depending on the availability of funds, new dresses are given.

Spiritual Development Services

The parents have permitted prayer in two of the tuition centres after two years. Few children come to Sunday worship service in the mission house. Children Picture Bibles in Odiya are distributed. Every month ten verses from Proverbs are printed and distributed to children. Plans to start Children Prayer Group in villages is underway since indifferences towards Christianity prevail in these areas.

Networking

FGF is open for initiating partnerships with local missions in Odisha. It is in regular contact with Child Evangelism Fellowship and Scripture Union office in Bhubaneswar for organizing children programs with the help of their staff.

Staff Capacity Building

Mission workers have attended field courses conducted by EFICOR. Weekly planning and review meetings are held.

Documentation

Educational capacity of each child is recorded for monitoring the progress. Health issues are noted down for follow up. Minutes of weekly work reviews are in place. Monthly reports on activities in connection to HCD are documented.

Sustainability

FGF is not supported by foreign funding. It functions as an interdenominational organization. Churches, prayer groups and families in Tamil Nadu are reached to share the vision of FGF. Three of FGF's mission workers are supported by two Lutheran churches and one Baptist church.

Parents of the children are encouraged to contribute in a minimum scale towards handouts like notebooks and dresses. They pay two rupees per child per month for tuition. Small savings schemes available with Post Office are introduced to the parents so that they will be able to participate in and contribute to the distribution of educational items for the children in future.

In the mission, field activities like farming and goat rearing are undertaken. It is hoped that in future these resources will be of valuable support to carry on activities.

Challenges

FGF engages young Christians from Odisha to coordinate tuition centres. It took two years to convince them that FGF does not receive any foreign money. The mission workers were brought to Chennai and other places to meet the supporters. They now understand how FGF raises funds.

It has been a challenge to train the mission workers on HCD. So far, they are familiar with ministering to children for spiritual development. They were initially sceptical about being involved in tutoring, caring for the sick, and providing secular books and newspapers for the children in the villages. It took time for them to be convinced that God wants us to go beyond evangelism to show the children and hence their parents that God cares for every aspect of their development.

Another challenge is to convince churches in Tamil Nadu that God wants us to have concern for the poor as a priority in our ministry and mission. FGF emphasises that sending a missionary and supporting his family alone is not adequate; Caring for people is also the concern of churches. While considering caring for people it should be borne in mind that we help them unconditionally, irrespective of their response to the gospel; because nobody knows when they will respond. Only the Lord of harvest knows and we are his servants tilling the land and sowing the seeds. The challenge of raising local leadership is being dealt with now. Churches located in cities like Sambalpur and Bhubaneswar are invited to participate in this mission by sending youth to teach the children school lessons, songs and plays.

Conclusion

Prem Parivar tuition centres are run for Odisha Ghasi children. At present there is no church in the villages where the centres are functioning. When churches emerge, these centres will be handed over to them.

9 789390 569083